KETO KIDS LUNCH BREAK

25 HEALTHY, DELICIOUS, EASY TO MAKE, SCHOOL-READY LUNCH AND SNACK RECIPES FOR YOUR CHILD ON THE GO

EVA ILIANA

CONTENTS

INTRODUCTION

HEALTHIER DIET OPTIONS FOR CHILDREN

Fig. 1: Unhealthy Eating, Unsplash, by Abigail Miller, 2018, https://unsplash.com/photos/r4zxIf0gTfs/ Copyright 2018 by Abigail Miller/Unsplash.

These days, children are often exposed to unhealthy food options both at home and in school. In the past, children could focus more on eating fruits, veggies, and other healthy foods because they were more readily available. Now, supermarkets, restaurants, and even school cafeterias have made unhealthy food options more abundant. Since these food items are full of additives that add to their flavors, these make them more appealing to children. But just because they taste better, this doesn't mean that they are healthier for children too.

When it comes to diet, parents in this modern-day world are struggling to get their kids to eat healthier throughout the day. Instead of eating processed, packaged or junk food all the time, it's better to encourage your kids to opt for healthier food options to make sure that they grow healthy, happy, and strong. However, doing this isn't as easy as it may seem, especially since unhealthy foods can be found everywhere you look! The good news is that this eBook will help you learn how to encourage your children to go for healthier diet options instead of the usual unhealthy treats they have gotten so used to.

Have you ever heard of the ketogenic diet?

If not, this is a specialized type of diet that involves eating high amounts of fat, moderate amounts of protein, and minimal amounts of carbs. As a parent, learning everything you can about the ketogenic diet and how you can use it for the benefit of your kids. In this eBook, I will present to you all the fundamental information you need to know about keto for kids along with a number of ketogenic recipes that your kids will love. Cooking these recipes for your children can serve as an excellent alternative to their school snacks and school lunches.

I myself am a parent of two girls and I have struggled with their diet, especially with the things they eat in school. Since I am also a working mother, I always succumbed to my busy schedule and I always felt like I didn't have any choice but to allow my girls to eat whatever was served in school. But whenever I asked my daughters what they would have for lunch or snacks in school, they would always tell me stories about eating junk food, fast food, and other food options that were generally unhealthy. Because of this, I made the conscious decision to make sure that my girls would eat healthily and learn how to make healthier choices at an early age and even when I am not around (like when they're in school).

In this day and age, parents are pressured to just give money to their kids and allow them to buy their own food. But if your child doesn't know what is healthy and what isn't, they will most likely opt for the same types of food their peers get. Unfortunately, most kids these days prefer junk food that contains a lot of unhealthy ingredients that can have adverse effects on their health. But as a firm believer in the power of food in our health, I also believe that making healthy choices has a trickle-down effect. If you can teach your children to always choose healthy food, this will make them feel better about themselves both mentally and physically.

So I did my research about the different kinds of diets and among all of them, the ketogenic diet caught my attention. I started following it and after some time, I started feeling better about my health. Then I did more research to find out if the ketogenic diet is suitable for kids too. I consulted with dieticians, nutritionists, and even my daughters' pediatrician. Although this diet does come with its own rules to follow, I worked together with these medical professionals and my daughters to start them on the high-fat, low-carb diet that is gaining popularity all over the world.

The thing I love about the ketogenic diet is that it promotes proper nutrition. When I introduced my girls to this diet, they started feeling the good effects too. Since I started following it before I encouraged them to follow suit, I was able to guide them through the process—what to eat, what to avoid, what they might feel when starting the diet, and so on. It is easier to encourage children to go keto when you've already been following it for some time but it's also possible to start following the ketogenic diet along with your children. As you will soon come to discover, the ketogenic diet will make your children healthier, happier, and it will even make your home life a lot easier.

Even if your children have been following the standard high-carb diet until now, that's okay. The great thing about healthy diets is that it's never too late to start following them. Think about it this way: a lot of people try changing their diets when they reach adulthood. So don't you think it would be even easier and more beneficial if you can encourage your children to follow a healthier diet while they are still young?

So now, here you are, reading a book about a specialized diet that most believe is only suitable for adults when the truth is, even children can thrive on keto as long as they follow it correctly. Later, I will be sharing with you the many benefits of the keto diet for children but for now, let me share an example with you that shows how this diet can be good for your little ones:

Let's say that your go-to breakfast option for your child is a bowl of cereal. So your child wakes up, eats their bowl of cereal, and goes to school. In school, your child sits in class listening to the teacher. At this point, your child's blood sugar level plummets which, in turn, make it difficult for them to keep their eyes open. This is because cereal is chock-full of carbs and sugar that rapidly increase sugar levels for about an hour or two. Then your child experiences a sugar crash that brings their energy levels down, too. But if you feed your child a low-carb, high-fat meal for breakfast, they will feel energized for the whole morning. Such a meal would also improve their focus, mood, and mental clarity, all of which will benefit them in school. The keto diet will make their minds sharper while giving them enough energy to get through the day without feeling tired or sleepy. This trend will continue as they are growing up as long as they continue following the keto diet correctly.

As I have mentioned, my girls are already experiencing the many benefits of the ketogenic diet. This is why I decided to write this book—to share everything I have learned and experienced with you and all other parents who are interested in encouraging their kids to go keto. Also, another main reason I wrote this book is to share with you some of the best, tastiest, and most fun recipes I have made with my daughters. Even if you have a picky eater, these recipes will be appealing to them. They're tasty, healthy, and really fun to make. One of the best ways for you to encourage your children to follow the keto diet is to involve them in your cooking. When they cook their own food, they learn how to appreciate their meals even more.

With my keto-for-kids expertise and my list of healthy recipes, your children will never crave junk foods for their snacks, lunches or dinners again. While the transition period might come with some challenges, try to remain positive. Going keto is a journey which means that it won't happen overnight. But as long as you keep trying, you keep encouraging, and you keep coming up with new and interesting dishes for your children, the journey can be one that will bring you closer while improving your health in the process.

While it's true that it is never too late to start eating healthier, there is still no better time to start than the present. It's time to start teaching your children how to eat healthier, especially since they are in their most impressionable years. It's also time for them to start breaking their unhealthy eating habits to give them a brighter, healthier future where they will carry with them the habits that you teach and experience the benefits that this diet has to offer. You have in your hands an eBook that will guide you to help your children become followers of the ketogenic diet just like you.

When you're done going through all of the practical information, tips, and strategies, you can start reading the different recipes so you know what to shop for the next time you go to the grocery store. Even if you're not a cooking master, the recipes in this eBook are so simple and easy that you can start making them after buying the required ingredients. With that being said, let's begin your child's keto journey!

1

WHY IS THERE SO MUCH HYPE SURROUNDING THE KETOGENIC DIET?

If you're interested in diets and health trends, then you would have probably heard or read about the ketogenic diet already. The ketogenic diet—keto for short—is one of the trendiest diets now and it's all about eating lots of fats, moderate

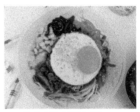

Fig. 2: Keto Bowl, Unsplash, by Markus Winkler, 2020, https://unsplash.com/photos/Ci5B4cnwEjwY/ Copyright 2020 by Markus Winkler/Unsplash.

amounts of protein, and restricting carbs. The first time people hear about this diet, they feel surprised because this time, bacon, butter, meat, oil, and the like are considered healthy.

While the keto diet has been around for quite some time now, it exploded in popularity when people discovered that it is an excellent diet for weight loss and, of course, that it allows you to eat high-fat foods that were previously believed to be unhealthy. But when you eat a lot of fat and restrict your carb intake, it can improve your health, boost your performance, sharpen your mind, and enhance your overall quality of life.

While this diet sounds like a dream come true, you might be wondering: doesn't my body need carbs?

The optimal carb intake depends on your gender, age, lifestyle, and other health factors. But when it comes to carbs, the type is more significant than the quality. Complex carbs like oatmeal, quinoa, and beans, for example, won't cause a quick rise in your blood sugar levels. Complex carbs also contain fiber, nutrients, and slow-burning energy making these healthier compared to simple carbs. Some examples of simple carbs are sugar, fruit concentrates, and syrups—all of which are commonly found in processed sweets and junk foods that are found in abundance in supermarkets, food shops, and even in school cafeterias. After eating these simple carbs, your sugar levels will spike significantly, thus giving you energy. But after a while, you will experience a sugar crash when your insulin levels drop as fast as they increased. Because of this, you would feel lethargic and weak, thus, pushing you to eat more to get the energy you need to get through your day.

Unfortunately, this kind of eating habit isn't the healthiest and it might even contribute to weight gain. This is why there are a lot of diets that encourage the minimization or restriction of carbs as this macronutrient has the most adverse health effects. One such diet is the ketogenic diet and as you will learn later, this diet has a lot of health benefits, even for children.

As you restrict your carb intake while following the keto diet, your body will start to eliminate excess water and sugar. This, in turn, causes weight loss, especially at the beginning. However, this diet does come with its risks and precautions which is why you should learn everything that you can about it first before you start following it or before you start encouraging your children to follow it too.

As I have mentioned, the ketogenic diet consists of high-fats, moderate proteins, and minimal carbs. For each meal, you are encouraged to consume around 1 to 2 thumb-sized portions of avocado, nuts, cheese, and other fat-dense foods. You can adjust this portion depending on your health goals, body size, and activity levels. The majority of your diet would consist of high-fat foods as these are the ones that will force your body into the state of ketosis. **For protein, you should consume at least 10% to 20% of your total intake each day.** This means that each meal should have a minimum of 20g of protein. To make the most of this macronutrient, it's best to focus on high-quality protein like fresh (not processed) meat, eggs, milk, cheese, and so on. Just make sure that you don't consume too much as this macronutrient can be converted into glucose which, in turn, brings ketosis to a halt. Finally, following the ketogenic diet means that you should only consume the bare minimum in terms of carbs. In other words, just enough to survive.

It might seem easy to follow but if you have been following the Standard American Diet in the past, going keto is a huge change. If your children are currently following the Standard American Diet and you plan to let them follow keto too, prepare yourself for the transition phase. There is a lot of hype surrounding the ketogenic diet and for good reason. This beneficial diet can potentially improve your life and the lives of your children, especially if you follow it correctly and consistently.

Is the Ketogenic Diet Suitable for Children?

The ketogenic diet is a specialized type of diet that has

become very trendy in recent years. In the beginning, it was developed to help patients suffering from epilepsy but since then, it has transformed and grew into a huge health trend that caught the attention of health, fitness, and wellness enthusiasts all over the world. Since you are reading this eBook right now, it means that you are interested in learning about the effects of keto on children and how you can use the diet to improve their health.

For adults, the ketogenic diet is relatively safe. As long as you follow it correctly and you consistently choose healthy keto-friendly options, this diet offers so many health benefits to improve your life. But when it comes to children, things aren't as simple. Most of the time, children should only follow this diet when prescribed by their doctor or to help them manage certain medical conditions.

Since the keto diet was first developed in the 1920s, it has been used as part of the treatment for children and adolescents who suffer from seizures and epilepsy. Back then, several studies had shown that the diet helped decrease the frequency of seizures in the patients by as much as 50%. The researchers believe that the anti-seizure effects of the diet come from the following factors:

- An increase in the consumption of brain-friendly antioxidants.
- An improvement in the metabolism of energy thanks to ketosis.
- A reduction in the excitability of the brain.

While the ketogenic diet is recommended for children who suffer from epilepsy and similar conditions, what about those who don't have any conditions? Those children who aren't suffering from any medical condition? Those children whose parents only want them to follow healthier diets to improve their health too?

For such children, the ketogenic diet may still be suitable—as long as you know how to guide your children through it. On average, children require about 130 grams of carbohydrates to maintain their health. However, for children who follow the Standard American Diet (most children in Western countries), they typically consume much more than 130 grams, especially when it comes to sugar. For adults who follow the ketogenic diet, they must consume less than 50 grams of carbs each day but this value must be adjusted based on the weight and height of your children.

Since the ketogenic diet focuses mostly on restricting carbs, this main feature is already beneficial for children. Encouraging your children to follow the keto diet means that you will be eliminating a lot of junk, sugary, and processed foods from their diets. Since these foods aren't healthy at all, this is already a huge plus. But if you really want your kids to go keto and enjoy all the potential benefits the diet has to offer, it's recommended that you focus on whole foods whether you're planning their fat, protein or carb sources.

For children, you don't have to be too strict when it comes to their carb intake, especially at the beginning. Also, if your children fall in the healthy weight range, this means that their insulin sensitivity is still adequate. Therefore, their bodies are still very effective in processing nutrient-dense carbs and sugars compared to the bodies of adults. But if your child is overweight and this is one of the main reasons why you have decided to start them on keto, then you may have to be more strict. Weight loss is a very common benefit of keto, thus, this diet is very helpful for children who are overweight. If your children can stick with the diet long-term, then they can maintain a healthy weight long-term too.

If you truly want your children to be healthy while following keto, you must stress the importance of whole foods as these will ensure their healthy growth and development. Minimizing your children's sugar and carb intake will be very beneficial and if you pair this with whole, keto-friendly foods, then they will be on their way to a healthy future. This is the main reason why it's also recommended for parents to learn how to prepare and cook keto-friendly meals and snacks. So that you can make sure that your children are only eating good food all day, every day.

If you want to ensure the safety of your children, then you can consult with their doctor first. Usually, your child will have to undergo preliminary lab work. The results will help you determine whether this diet will be safe for your children. When the results show that your children are suitable for the diet, then you can consult with a dietitian. This is an important step as a dietitian can provide you with all the information you need about the best types of food to feed your child and the keto variation that is most suitable for them too. After going through all of these steps, you can feel more confident about starting your children on the diet safely. It's also a good idea to continue consultations with your children's doctor to keep track of their health as they are following the diet. This is an effective way to make sure that their health and safety are always prioritized.

Keep in mind that the bodies of children are constantly growing and developing. Therefore, it is essential for you to always feed the nutrient-dense foods at every meal. This ensures that the complex mechanisms within their body continue functioning as they are growing up. Ensuring the health of your children while they are still young will also help ensure their health in the future.

As a parent, it's your responsibility to guide your children and teach them the proper habits to follow when it comes to their diet. While it's much easier to allow them to give in to the temptation of sweets, junk foods, and highly-processed foods, teaching these proper habits while your children are still young will make healthy choices come naturally to them. Then even when you're not around, like when they're at school, they will continue making healthy choices instead of giving in to their peers.

Although this won't be the easiest thing to do, getting your children to go keto is not an impossible task. This diet is suitable for children even as they are growing and developing. Around this time, they are also developing food preferences. So when you get your children used to eating healthy foods, these are the types of food that they will continue eating even into adulthood. To encourage your children, you have to create a plan for how you will introduce the diet and let them follow it. Staying positive throughout the process will prove to be more effective than immediately restricting certain food groups as this might cause your children to resent the diet instead of appreciating it.

Also, remember that following this diet will impact the cultural experiences of your children. While eating at home, your children will enjoy the same meals as you and the rest of your family. But when they go to school, they will have to be strong enough to follow their diet even if their peers might have a lot of questions for them. This becomes easier for your children if you encourage them and highlight all the benefits the ketogenic diet has to offer. The more positive your children feel about the diet, the more they will continue following it no matter what. The good news is that throughout this book, you will learn how to guide your children in the best possible ways.

WHAT ARE THE BENEFITS OF THE KETOGENIC DIET FOR CHILDREN?

The ketogenic diet is a unique diet that can offer some specific medical benefits to those who suffer from specific medical issues. For people of all ages, this diet can help bring normalcy to their lives by improving their health. All over the world, the ketogenic diet is still being used as part of the treatment for different conditions. But as we have established, even healthy children can follow this diet under your guidance as a parent.

While the ketogenic diet may seem pretty simple, it's not all about eliminating all carbs from your kids' diets and feeding them with fat bombs, bacon, and fried foods. You should also learn how to balance your children's diets by giving them healthy fats, proteins, and carbs. In doing this, you can increase the likelihood of your children experiencing the health benefits the ketogenic diet has to offer. But with research, planning, and a little bit of creativity, getting your children to follow the ketogenic diet can become easier.

Did you know that we all started our lives on the keto diet? Breastfed babies are considered to be in the natural state of ketosis. This is because breast milk mainly contains fat and it is specifically designed to meet all the nutrient needs of babies who are rapidly growing and developing. This is a fact. Now, if you try to think about it, if we followed the keto diet while we were infants and it made us grow big and strong, isn't it safe to assume that allowing children to follow the ketogenic diet correctly is safe too?

Yes, it is. But it's not as simple as that. As a parent, you must learn how to administer this diet correctly to ensure the safety of your children and to give them the following benefits:

It encourages children to make healthier food choices

When it comes to the ketogenic diet, your most important role as a parent is to teach your children to have a healthier relationship with food and you can do this by encouraging the consumption of whole, healthy foods while following the diet. One of the more traditional aspects of the ketogenic diet is that it encourages the consumption of fruits and vegetables. However, not all fruits and veggies are suitable for this diet. Many fruits and veggies contain high amounts of sugar and starch—and these are the ones that you should either limit or avoid.

For instance, mangoes, bananas, and grapes have a lot of sugar. After all, this is why fruits are called nature's candy. If your children love fruits, then you may have to find other sweet treats that are more suitable for them. But when it comes to limiting sweets or carbs, you can start with the unhealthy options like sugar, candies, and other high-sweet desserts. Then if they really want something sweet and you haven't prepared anything, giving them fruit won't be the worst thing in the world. Over time, your children will get used to their low-sugar and low-carb diet and when this happens, you can start weaning them off fruits too.

As for vegetables, most types are suitable for the diet. While there are vegetables like potatoes, beans, and corn that are high in starch, the list of keto-friendly vegetables is much longer. For this diet, focus on feeding your children green, leafy vegetables and adding all the other types of low-carb veggies to various dishes.

Although veggies and fruits are very healthy, the stars of the keto diet are meat and healthy fats. There aren't a lot of fatty fruits or vegetables which is why you would only include them in your children's meals as side dishes or additional ingredients. Then you would focus more on fish, meat, and poultry to create dishes that will make your kids happy, healthy, and satisfied.

It allows children to consume the protein they need to grow

Since the ketogenic diet encourages the consumption of meat, you can be sure that your children will get the protein they need to grow big and strong. For this diet, a child who weighs 50-pounds should consume between 100g to 150g of protein each day while consuming more fats. The great thing about protein is that it's filling, thus, there is a very small chance that your children will overeat. Still, try to make sure that your children won't eat excessive amounts of protein as it might hinder ketosis, which is the main benefit of the ketogenic diet.

It helps stabilize your children's blood sugar levels

When children follow the Standard American Diet, their parents have to keep up with their erratic energy levels. Eating foods that are high in carbs and sugar will cause a continuous increase and decrease of energy levels which, in turn, may lead to attention and behavior issues.

Try to observe your children before you start them on keto. You will notice that after eating, they tend to be so hyperactive, especially when the meal they consumed is high in carbs and sugar. Now, try to imagine what happens in school after lunch when all children just consumed their high-carb meals.

How will they focus on their tasks or follow directions when they're hopped up on sugar?

But after a few hours have passed, your children will start experiencing a sugar crash wherein they are much calmer. In school, the students become much easier to control, however, some of them still find it difficult to concentrate because they don't have enough energy! Whether at home or in school, this continuous spike and drop of blood sugar levels can be very challenging to deal with.

If your child is following the ketogenic diet, you won't have to worry about this roller coaster of energy. Since the diet focuses more on fats and protein, your children's sugar levels will remain stable throughout the day. This stability can also prevent the development of insulin resistance which, in turn, reduces the risk of diabetes, heart disease, fatty liver, and other serious illnesses.

It may help your children lose weight when needed

The weight loss benefit of the ketogenic diet is the most common and most popular reason why people start following it. But for children, this isn't a major benefit. After all, most parents want their children to gain weight while they are growing up. If your children are at a healthy weight, don't focus too much on the portion or caloric-restriction aspect of the diet. In fact, it's better to make sure that your children are getting all the calories they need through their meals and snacks even if you are restricting certain foods from their diets.

But in the case of overweight or obese children, this is a significant benefit you can look forward to. This benefit comes from the very nature of the diet. When the body is starved of carbs and sugar, it shifts into a metabolic state known as ketosis. When this happens, the body starts burning fat for fuel instead of glucose. The longer the body is in ketosis, the more fat it burns. For overweight or obese children, this means that their bodies will start burning their fat stores too. Over time, you may notice that your children are losing weight as you continue to encourage them to follow keto.

Now, here is the challenge. When it comes to keto for kids, you might not be able to restrict their carb intake as much as you do with yourself. To handle your children's carb intake more effectively, opt for nutrient-dense and fibrous carb sources. That way, even if your children are eating more carbs than what is recommended, at least they are eating healthy carbs. Some examples of healthy carbs you can feed your children are nuts, hummus, Greek yogurt, string cheese, and fruit. These carb-rich foods are much better than low-nutrient carbs like chips, cookies, pasta, and rice. To help your child lose weight on this diet, learn how to make smarter replacements so you don't have to make your children feel like you are restricting them severely.

For this benefit, there is one precaution I would like to share. If you are starting your children on keto when they are in their pre-teen or teen years, be very careful with how you introduce and encourage them to follow the diet, especially if they are obese or overweight. Pre-teens and teens tend to be very sensitive and if they misinterpret your efforts to make their lives healthier, they might develop an eating disorder. Of course, you wouldn't want this to happen. This is why it's important to make the whole experience positive. Focus on the health aspect of the diet so your children understand that you are encouraging them to follow the diet to become healthier and avoid illnesses.

It is safe for children as long as you follow it correctly

There are ways for you to ensure your children's safety while following keto. As long as you follow the very precise rules of this diet, your children can experience the benefits and not the potential side effects. Also, following a healthy diet such as this will help protect your children from the side effects of processed, high-carb food that are readily available no matter where you look.

Your children will enjoy the health benefits even when they grow up

Finally, if your children will follow this diet long-term, they will continue experiencing the health benefits even as they grow up. While your children are growing up, you can make adjustments to their diet to accommodate the nutritional needs. The older your children get, the more you can explain the diet to them until the day when they can start making their own healthy choices without your guidance.

As you can see, the ketogenic diet does offer a number of health benefits for children. These are the most significant ones but if you research keto for adults, you will see that this diet offers many more benefits. But the key here is to make sure that you follow the diet correctly. Just like any other diet, keto has its own rules which are based on the original ketogenic plan that was developed years ago. Although some of the rules may have changed, the basic ones still exist and these are the ones that promote the good effects of the diet on the health of your children.

2

HOW DO YOU GET YOUR CHILD TO START EATING HEALTHY?

Fig. 3: Eating Healthy. Unsplash, by Tanaphong Toochinda, 2019, link
https://unsplash.com/photos/FEhPttQdLYsM/ Copyright 2019 by
Tanaphong Toochinda/Unsplash.

Now that you know more about the ketogenic diet specifically for children, you may start creating a plan for how you will encourage your children to follow it. Before you introduce the diet to your child, it's recommended to have them evaluated by their doctor. This evaluation involves a complete physical examination along with the required lab tests. Then you would also have to share your child's diet history including their food preferences, what food they don't like, what food you typically serve at home, their normal food portions, whether you have trouble feeding them certain types of food, and if your family has any food restrictions because of religion or culture. All of this information is important so that your child's doctor can determine if it's suitable for them to follow the ketogenic diet.

If your child suffers from any medical condition that

requires them to go keto, they would have to stay in the hospital when you start the diet. Typically, they would have to spend 5 to 8 days in the hospital where they will be introduced to the high-fat, low-carb diet. After your child has begun the diet, their doctor might request for urine and blood samples to check for ketone levels. These samples will be taken at regular intervals along with your child's blood sugar levels. All of these things will happen while your child is in the hospital so their doctor can monitor them while their body is adjusting to the new diet. If needed, your child will also be given supplements to maintain the balance in their body. During these first few days, your child may feel tired or may even experience some side effects like nausea, vomiting, and low levels of blood sugar. Since your child will be at the hospital, their doctor will be able to monitor their condition and make adjustments as needed.

But if your child isn't suffering from any kind of medical condition and you just want them to follow a healthier diet, it's still recommended that you have them checked to ensure that they can follow the diet safely. Throughout the process mentioned above, the hospital stay may be omitted but this depends on your child's doctor. If your child's doctor recommends that you start the diet in the hospital so your child can be monitored, then it's best to listen. If not, make sure that you have done your research and you have a solid plan for how you will introduce keto to your child. Aside from reading resources about keto for kids like this book, it would be helpful to talk to your child's doctor and even a nutritionist who specializes in diets for children. Doing this will give you a good idea of how you will properly introduce keto along with all of its strict rules.

Since the ketogenic diet consists of high amounts of fat, moderate amounts of protein, and low amounts of carbs, following it will change the body's metabolism. When you restrict your child from eating carbs, their body won't have enough to burn for energy. Therefore, their body will be forced into ketosis wherein it starts burning fat for fuel. When your child enters ketosis, ketones will be found in their blood or urine which is why tests are done in the hospital to check these levels. If you choose not to hospitalize your child while you start the diet, you may bring them to the doctor to check their ketone levels regularly.

Since your child is probably used to following a high-carb diet, you shouldn't restrict their carb intake right away or too drastically. Start slowly by introducing the diet, explaining the changes that will take place, and the reasons for these changes (the potential benefits of the diet). This is where your planning will come in handy. Think about what types of food your child normally eats and try to determine which ones to eliminate first. For instance, if your child loves eating cake, sugary pastries, and sweet cereals, think about which of these foods you want to limit first. Over time, you can increase the types of food that you limit depending on how well your child is adjusting to the diet.

You should follow the most current dietary guidelines for children even if you're letting them follow a restrictive diet like keto. According to these guidelines, your child's carb intake should account for 45% to 65% of their daily total. Of course, this is quite high for keto since it is a low-carb diet. When making calculations, you should mainly consider your child's age and gender. Generally, though, the recommended daily intake of carbs for healthy children are:

- 110g to 159g per day for children ages 1 to 3 years old.

- 130g to 220g per day for children ages 4 to 8 years old.
- 170g to 280g per day for children ages 9 to 14 years old.
- 220g to 300g per day for children ages 14 to 18 years old.

Make sure to follow these recommendations to ensure that your child is getting enough carbs to keep them healthy. Over time, you can reduce your child's carb intake until you reach the most ideal level to kick their body into ketosis. In the meantime, while you still allow them to eat carbs, always opt for healthy carbs like fruits, grains, and dairy as opposed to letting them eat pastries, pasta or bread.

Normally, you would allow your child to follow the ketogenic diet for up to two years before you start shifting them back to the Standard American Diet. This time, though, your child should be more used to eating healthier foods even while following a regular diet. But if you see that the diet is doing your child a lot of good, you may choose to continue the diet for as long as it is still beneficial for them. But if the diet is part of your child's treatment plan, then you should consult with their doctor first before you choose to either stop the diet or continue it.

Introducing the Ketogenic Diet to Children

Introducing any new diet to children isn't a simple thing. If your child is used to a certain diet and they have been following that diet from the beginning, asking them to follow new eating habits or try out new types of food can be quite challenging. But as long as you remain consistent and you don't give up, you will find success. When it's time to start, prepare yourself for it. Expect to spend a lot of time explaining the diet to your child, showing them how to follow the diet, and learning how to make keto-friendly meals for your child and the rest of the family.

The great thing about this diet is that you can customize it according to your child's needs and how well they are adjusting to the diet. If your child is struggling, give them time. But if you see that your child is very interested in the diet (thanks to the delicious meals you cook for them), then you can continue with it. Here are a few more tips to help you introduce the ketogenic diet to your child successfully:

1. Start as soon as possible

After you have learned everything you can about the diet and you have already consulted with your child's doctor, you can start guiding your child into it. The earlier you can introduce the ketogenic diet to your child, the better. It is especially helpful if you can introduce this diet when their food preferences are forming. That way, your child will get a preference for keto-friendly foods instead of foods that are high in carbs and sugar. Introduce different types of keto-friendly foods regularly and see how your child reacts to them. If they don't like the food, try again at some other time. But if they have a good reaction to the foods you give them, keep going!

2. Show your children how to follow the diet

It would be much easier for you to encourage your child to follow the ketogenic diet if you follow it too. Take my situation, for instance. I started following the ketogenic diet a few months before introducing it to my girls. Since I was already following the diet, I was able to share my own experiences with my daughters as they started their keto journeys. So whenever I cooked meals or presented food to them, I was always the first one to taste. Then they would feel more motivated to give those foods a try too. Apart from showing your child how to follow the ketogenic diet, here are some ways for you to encourage them and keep them motivated:

- Praise your child if they willingly try out new foods.
- Expose your child to a variety of new and healthy foods.
- Encourage your whole family to follow the same diet so that your child sees exactly what it means to eat healthily.

3. Choose what to feed your child wisely

As a parent, you will be the one who decides what ingredients to buy and what meals or snacks to serve your child. In the beginning, your child might complain or beg you for the sugary, salty, and generally unhealthy foods that they are used to. It may be easier to give in, but at the end of the day, you still make the final decision. Instead of feeding your child with ready-made, processed foods (even if they claim to be keto-friendly), prepare your child's meals and snacks using fresh, whole ingredients. That way, you always have something to serve to your child whenever they feel hungry.

4. Go slow

It's never a good idea to give your child a shock by suddenly clearing out your pantry and refrigerator only leaving behind foods that are new and unfamiliar to them. If you do this, you might intimidate your child too much which, in turn, might make them dislike the diet. Instead, go slow by gradually eliminating refined or processed carbs while starting to introduce healthy fats (like nuts, coconut oil, avocado oil) and healthy protein sources (like eggs, fish, poultry, meat). Also, get your child used to eating leafy greens and other non-starchy veggies. Every 2 to 3 days, eliminate a new type of food then introduce a new type of food to replace it. This makes it easier for your child to ease into the diet.

5. Give your child gateway foods

Gateway foods are foods that are familiar to your child. Combining new foods with these gateway foods makes it easier for your child to accept the new food. For instance, if your child loves eating fish, you can whip up healthy, keto-friendly fish dishes while introducing new vegetables to their diet. When you do this, your child will associate the new vegetables with the food that they love which, in this example, is fish. This is where your creativity comes in. Try to think of your child's favorite foods and use these as gateway foods to introduce new and unfamiliar food items to them.

6. Involve your child in preparing and cooking food

This tip is highly effective and lots of fun for children. When you involve your child in preparing and cooking their food, they will be more willing to taste those foods. Allowing your child to help you prepare and cook meals—and even go shopping for ingredients—exposes them to a variety of foods which, in turn, makes them more interested. Remember that children have a natural curiosity. Use this when you are introducing the ketogenic diet.

Trust me, this can be a lot of fun for you too. Ever since I allowed my children to cook with me, they have always shown willingness to try new things. I show them new ingredients, allow them to taste while we cook, and, of course, we happily share the meals and snacks that we prepare together. Cooking with your child doesn't just make the diet easier... It also creates a unique bonding routine for you and your child that brings you closer while contributing to your health too.

7. Make sure that your child is well hydrated

One of the most effective ways to ensure success on the ketogenic diet is to make sure that your child is always well-hydrated. Drinking enough water also helps your children avoid the most common side effects of the ketogenic diet. When it comes to sufficient water intake, here are the recommendations:

For girls

- 1.7 liters of water each day for children ages 4 to 8 years old.
- 2.1 liters of water each day for children ages 9 to 13 years old.
- 2.3 liters of water each day for children ages 14 to 18 years old.
- 2.7 liters of water each day for children aged 19 and above.

For young boys

- 1.7 liters of water each day for children ages 4 to 8 years old.
- 2.4 liters of water each day for children ages 9 to 13 years old.
- 3.3 liters of water each day for children ages 14 to 18 years old.
- 3.7 liters of water each day for children aged 19 and above.

If your child leads a very active lifestyle, then you may want to increase their water intake so that they don't end up getting dehydrated.

8. Don't force them into anything

This is one of the most important things to keep in mind when introducing a new diet to your child. Remember that it's better to encourage your child instead of forcing them so that they learn to love the diet instead of resenting it. Accept the fact that your child might not want some of the keto-friendly foods you introduce. Sometimes, they might not even like the meals or snacks you cook for them. This is okay. As long as you don't give up and you keep trying to encourage them to eat keto-friendly foods, they will eventually learn to love these foods. Introducing keto is even more challenging if you have a picky eater. If you're having challenges, go back to the other tips I have shared in this chapter. These are very practical tips which, hopefully, can help you introduce keto to your child successfully.

When it comes to introducing the ketogenic diet, the bottom line is for you to make a plan then enjoy the experience. Use your plan as a guide but allow for flexibility too. You are trying to change your child's life for the better so try not to get discouraged. Just keep encouraging your child and making things interesting so that they have fun following the diet and they get the motivation they need to keep going.

Tips for Getting Children to Follow the Ketogenic Diet

The famous ketogenic diet offers a lot of good things for the health of children. After introducing the diet to your child, make sure that you keep encouraging them to follow it until they have made it a part of their life. Whether your child accepts the diet easily at the beginning or it takes some time for them to agree to it, continuing with the diet is important, especially if you want your child to experience the potential health benefits. Encouraging your child to follow keto will involve a lot of trial and error moments. The longer you stick with it, the more you will learn. You will learn more about your child, their true preferences and eating habits, which tips and strategies work for them, and which don't. To help make things easier for you, here are a few tips that have worked wonders for me to encourage your child to continue with their keto journey:

1. Teach your child new cooking skills while they follow the diet

Involving your child in the meal prep and cooking process is a lot of fun. This activity allows you to bond with your child and it makes them happier to follow the diet since they will be preparing and cooking their own food. But if you do the same thing over and over again, your child might get bored. When this happens, they might lose interest in cooking and the diet. So just like the diet itself, you should try mixing up the cooking skills you teach. There are so many cooking skills to learn like:

- measuring ingredients,
- tossing salads,
- slicing meat, fruits or vegetables,
- stirring dry or liquid mixtures,
- kneading dough,
- and so much more.

Think about the dishes you plan to make for the week and read the recipes for how to make them. That way, you can mix and match the recipes and ingredients so that cooking is always a fun and pleasant experience that leads to their meals. Of course, if your child is younger, then you may have to take more time when cooking as they won't move as quickly or as efficiently as older kids. Make sure to assign age-appropriate skills to your child so they don't end up getting overwhelmed or frustrated while helping you.

2. Allow your child to make their own plate

Although cooking is a fun activity, you don't have to involve your child at every meal. Imagine how much time you would need for cooking if your child helps you make breakfast, lunch, and dinner each day. For those times when your child didn't help you cook the meal, you can allow them to make their own plate. To do this, lay out all of the keto-friendly dishes you have prepared and give them an empty plate. Allow your child to choose which foods to place on their plate. This is another way of involving your child in the process of preparing their food which, in turn, motivates them to keep following the diet despite the introduction of new and unfamiliar food.

3. Allow your child to make their own choices

When you don't give your child a choice, it will soon feel like you are forcing them to follow the ketogenic diet. This is a big no-no as it will decrease the willingness and motivation of your child to try new things. Just as you would allow your child to make their own plate at every meal, allow them to freely choose what food to eat. Just make sure that everything you offer them is keto-friendly so that whatever choice they make would be the right choice.

This tip doesn't just apply to breakfast, lunch, and dinner. For instance, when you're meal planning, involve your child too. Print out pictures of the recipes you have gathered and allow them to choose which ones you will cook throughout the week. When it comes to snacks, you can buy or prepare a variety of snacks for them and when they feel hungry, allow them to choose which snack to eat. The mere act of allowing your child to choose freely will make them feel happy and excited. Then maybe the diet can be a lot easier for you and your child too!

4. Teach your child to focus on healthy foods

As you are encouraging your child to go keto and you do this by involving them as much as possible with the diet, you would also be teaching them to focus on healthy foods. It isn't just about buying healthy foods, it's also about getting rid of unhealthy foods that you may have stored in your home. If you had followed the Standard American Diet in the past, chances are, you still have a lot of processed, sugary, high-carb foods in your pantry or cupboards.

As part of your keto journey, make it a point to rid your home of these non-keto food options. That way, your child won't get tempted by them. You don't have to throw these things out. You can give them to your friends or family or you can even donate them to shelters. When your home is free of unhealthy food, then you can teach your child to focus on foods that are good for their health.

5. Encourage your child to snack smarter

All children love snacks and sometimes, it seems like they can just keep snacking throughout the day! The good news is that this doesn't have to be a problem while on keto. There are so many keto-friendly snack options your child can indulge in. These days, most food shops offer snacks that are suitable for the ketogenic diet. You can feed these snacks to your child even when you're on-the-go. Of course, if you want to stick with homemade, healthier food, then you can prepare your child's snacks from home.

Later, you will learn how to make a number of sweet and savory snacks to make for your child. After practicing with the simple recipes in this eBook, you can search for more complex recipes online to make things interesting. When you and your child have become master snack-makers, you can even come up with your own fun snacks using keto-friendly ingredients! There are even some keto snack options that require no preparation at all like cottage cheese, sugar-free peanut butter, and sliced veggies with guacamole dip, for example. When it comes to snacking, bring out your innovation and creativity to keep your child inspired to follow the diet consistently along with the rest of the family.

6. Don't forget fiber!

If there's one thing that typically gets neglected when following the ketogenic diet, it's fiber. The main sources of fiber are fruits and vegetables but the diet recommends that you limit certain types of fruits and vegetables as they contain high amounts of sugar or starch. Most types of grains are also to be eliminated from the diet which means that your child might not get enough fiber.

Unfortunately, when the body doesn't get enough fiber, this may increase the risk of developing heart disease, obesity, and even colon cancer. Also, your child might experience constipation if they don't get enough fiber in their diet. To avoid these issues, make sure that your child's meals always contain something fiber-rich like avocados, seeds, and nuts. You may even ask your child's pediatrician if your child needs to take fiber supplements each day.

7. Encourage your child to try different veggies

As I have mentioned, most vegetables are suitable for the ketogenic diet since there are very few types that contain high amounts of carbs or sugar. Since you will be eliminating several types of fruits from your child's diet, you may want to increase their veggie intake to ensure that they are always properly nourished. Unfortunately, it's a lot easier to feed fruits to children than it is to convince them to eat their greens. Even if your child is following a regular diet, getting them excited to eat veggies can be a challenge. Just like any other food, though, there are things you can do to make it easier for yourself and your child:

- When you're introducing a new type of vegetable to your child, include it in their meals at least once a week. Even if your child won't like it the first time, feeding the same vegetable to them regularly will get them used to it. Also, if you use the vegetable as an ingredient in different dishes, you might discover one dish that your child really likes which includes the vegetable. Then this can be your go-to dish for when you want your child to eat that particular veggie.
- Prepare vegetables in a flavorful way. There are so many ways you can present vegetables to make them more appealing and interesting to eat. For instance, you can make zoodles out of zucchini, mashed cauliflower instead of mashed potato, vegetable casserole with cheese, and more. One day, you might be surprised when your child asks for these veggies dishes because they truly like the taste!
- When serving salads, vegetable sticks, and other vegetable dishes that aren't flavored with spices or sauces, pair these with keto-friendly flavorings like cream cheese and butter. Then give your child the choice to flavor their vegetables as they wish.
- Encourage your child to try everything that you

serve them. Even if your child doesn't like it, appreciate the fact that they gave it a try. Then, you can ask your child if they want to dip the vegetable in something they like to mask the actual taste of the veggie. For instance, if they want to smother it in sauce, let them. If they want to use some kind of dip, give them the dip. At least this shows that they are willing to continue eating the vegetable by combining it with something else to make it more palatable to them.

- If you discover a particular vegetable that your child likes, tell your child to load up on that veggie. For instance, if you cook a really tasty broccoli dish and your child loves it, tell them to load up. Then the next time you serve broccoli in the form of a different dish, remind your child how much they enjoyed broccoli the last time and encourage them to try this dish too. Often, convincing your child to eat their veggies involves some psychological tricks to make things easier.

When your child has already gotten used to eating different kinds of vegetables, take things a step further by allowing them to help you prepare their lunchboxes. If you want your child to continue going keto even at school, then it's better to pack their lunch instead of giving them money to buy food from the cafeteria. Do this consistently at least at the beginning of their keto journey. Give your child a couple of vegetable options and allow them to pick which one to include in their lunchbox. That way, your child will be more willing to eat everything in their lunchbox since they picked the contents themselves.

8. Make things fun for your child

Just as children learn more effectively when they are having fun, you can make their keto journey easier when you make things fun for them. As you may have noticed, the tips that I have already shared are child-centered—involving them in the cooking process, allowing them to choose their food, encouraging them to try new things. Applying these things in a positive way can help make the ketogenic diet more enjoyable for your child.

You can take things further by coming up with ways to make the diet more interesting. Some suggestions are:

- Thinking of games that involve their meals like "surprise snacks" or "surprise dinner" where you ask them to guess what they will eat by using their senses.
- Making a game out of the cooking process.
- Creating themed meals or snacks.
- Learning how to make bento boxes that showcase characters and other cute things to present your child's meals.

Your creativity will once again come into play here. If you're struggling to find ways to make things fun for your child, research online and you're sure to find a wealth of ideas to keep you busy and to keep your child interested in the diet.

When it comes to getting your child to stick with the ketogenic diet, you may have to put in a lot of time and effort into the task. You can't just explain the diet to your child and expect that they will follow it without issues. After all, even adults can sometimes face challenges while on keto. But with your guidance, your child will be able to stick with this new way of eating long-term. To round off this chapter, let me share with you a few final tips to keep in mind:

- As much as possible, prepare all of your child's meals and snacks from home. Sometimes, processed food products that are labeled as keto-friendly aren't healthy.
- Children love experiments. Use this fact to your advantage by thinking of ways to make food preparation seem like a long, ongoing experiment where you help them learn all about improving their health through the food they eat.
- When preparing your child's meals, try to make them as colorful and visually appealing as possible. Even if you're serving vegetables, making colorful meals will encourage your child to eat them without hesitation.
- One clever way to get your child to eat veggies is by making smoothies with a combination of fruits and vegetables. You can even throw in some nuts and berries to make your smoothies healthier.
- To help wean your child off sweets, have them eat one fruit each day. Try to choose fruits that are low on the glycemic index so that they can still satisfy their sweet tooth without deviating from the diet.
- When making sweet pastries and treats for your child Monk fruit is one of the best and safest sweeteners to use. With this sweetener, you can make cookies, cakes, cupcakes, and other sweets that are completely keto-friendly.
- While chicken is the most popular meat for children, you can replace this with other types of meat like fish, lamb, and veal to increase their omega-3 intake. Such meats are also easy to digest so your child won't have to experience tummy troubles.
- If your child constantly refuses nutrient-dense foods like eggs, seafood or liver, look for ways to mask these food items. For instance, you can make your

own mayonnaise using eggs or even liver pate to pair with bread. The more creative you can be, the more you can encourage your child to follow this diet.

- When choosing dairy products for your child, try to avoid cow's milk as it contains A1 casein that tends to increase inflammation and indigestion. Instead, opt for other dairy products like sheep or goat's milk when giving your child dairy.
- As much as possible, try to eat the same meals and snacks as your child. Remember my tip about showing your child how to follow the diet? This is extremely effective as most children love emulating adults. If your child sees you eating healthy foods, they are most likely to make the same healthy choices too.

Finally, try to develop a supportive and positive relationship with your child throughout the diet. This is very important so your child doesn't feel negative about the diet and, more importantly, so they won't risk developing an eating disorder because of it. Use encouragement, inspiration, and rewards as much as you can so that your child will feel happy about their new diet from the start.

3

THE GOOD SIDE AND BAD SIDE OF
KETO FOR CHILDREN

Compared to the other trendy diets that are sweeping the globe, the ketogenic diet is one of the most effective in terms of providing real benefits to those who follow it. This is probably because it was carefully devel-

Fig. 4: Good and Bad. Pixabay, by avitalchn, 2016, https://pixabay.com/photos/child-kids-children-food-eating-1566470/ Copyright 2016 by avitalchn/Pixabay.

oped as part of the treatment for epilepsy. Over the years, the keto diet has been studied, researched, and further developed to make it safe, effective, and beneficial even for healthy individuals. Despite being a very effective diet, keto does come with its downsides, precautions, and risks. This is why I always emphasize the fact that you have to follow the ketogenic diet correctly in order for it to become effective. In this chapter, we will discuss the good and bad side of the ketogenic diet. This is valuable information for you to learn so that you can make the best choices for your child.

Most children love eating high-carb, sugary, and generally unhealthy meals and snacks. But when you start them on the keto diet, then you would be eliminating most of these foods from their diet and replacing these with healthy fats and proteins in proper amounts. The great thing about following the ketogenic diet in this modern-day and age is that there are so many alternatives available. Due to the high popularity of the diet, the food industry has created keto-friendly options for virtually all kinds of snacks and treats. If you want to make all of your child's meals yourself (which I strongly recommend), then you can go online to search for recipes for keto meals, snacks, and desserts. Later, you will already learn a number of stellar recipes to start with and trust me, those recipes will surely make you popular with your child.

The most significant change you will be making to your child's diet is the restriction of carbs. However, this also happens to be the most significant drawback of the ketogenic diet. Children need carbs to grow and develop normally which is why you should be very careful when administering the diet to your child. For your child, you shouldn't eliminate all carbs from their diet. Not only will this interfere with their growth and development, but it will also make them feel weak. Also, your child might experience the other potential side effects of the diet if you don't follow it correctly or if you try to do too many things too fast. For adults, I would recommend that you listen to your body while starting the diet but when it comes to your child, communicate often with them so you know if the diet is making them feel better or not.

Going slow with the keto diet is important for children. That way, you don't cause shock to their body which, in turn, might make them reluctant to continue with it. Also, you should make sure that your child doesn't experience the more severe side effects like weak bones, high cholesterol and triglyceride levels, kidney stones, and nutritional deficiencies. Aside from monitoring your child carefully while following the diet, monitoring your child's health along with their doctor can help prevent these side effects from occurring. Here are a few important considerations for you when starting your child on keto:

- Remember that this is a restrictive type of diet which means that you will have to control the type of food your child will eat. Also, if you want your child to lose weight, you can control their portions too, although this isn't recommended for children.
- You may have to guide your child in terms of how they will continue following the diet even at school. Since your child will be on a specialized diet, they might feel isolated as they cannot eat what the other kids are eating. Explain why you have decided to start them on this diet and highlight the potential benefits to help your child understand. Your goal here is to ensure your child that the diet is for their own good and it's okay for them to eat different types of food.
- Planning, preparing, and cooking meals for the keto diet takes time, especially if you don't have previous experience with it. If you allow your child to help you out while cooking, the process will take even longer. So you may want to come up with a new schedule for your routine that allows you to create ketogenic meals for your child and the rest of your family.
- If you want your child to follow the ketogenic diet to help them overcome a medical condition, you should know that there is still a chance that it won't benefit your child no matter how closely they follow the

diet. As with any other diets, keto works well for some but it might not work for others. If your child has been following the diet for some time and you don't see any improvements, talk to your child's doctor about changing their diet or eating plan.

- One great thing about keto is that you can customize it to be suitable for any kind of ethnic diet. Even if your child has food intolerances or allergies, you can customize the diet to accommodate these. Since you will be the one who chooses what your child will eat, then it's up to you to customize their diet as needed.

The ketogenic diet has the potential to improve your child's life in so many ways. If you have already started on this diet, you should know what I am talking about. After all, if you had negative experiences with keto, you wouldn't allow your child to follow the same diet, right? Since this diet will change your child's body and metabolism, make sure to:

Keep your child active

This is especially important if you want your child to shed a few pounds. Instead of focusing only on restricting their caloric intake, encourage your child to exercise, play sports, and remain active too. If your child doesn't like sports, find something they would be more willing to do like dancing, swimming, skating or cycling, for example. That way, you can only focus on the types of food to restrict, not so much on portion control.

Let your child follow a well-balanced diet

Although healthy fats are the main focus of the keto diet, you should still make sure that your child is getting all the nutrients they need to stay healthy. After making sure that your child's meals contain enough healthy fats, plan for the protein, fiber, calcium, and even carb content of their meals. Also, make sure that your child is getting the essential vitamins and minerals from their diet too.

Limit your child's consumption of sugar and processed food

This is the key that will unlock your child's health. Sadly, these types of foods are very appealing to children although they have no nutritional value and they can even lead to health problems. Start eliminating these foods at home then you can talk to your child's teacher to just watch over your child and guide them so that they continue making wise food choices in school.

Diversify your child's meals

If you are going to eliminate foods from your child's diet, you should also replace them with other foods. As a parent, you should know what foods are suitable for the ketogenic diet and what foods aren't. This enables you to plan meals better and it improves your ability to mix and match ingredients and food items to make your child's diet more interesting. While your child will surely have favorite keto dishes, diversifying their diet will help make their transition smoother and easier.

THE ADVANTAGES OF LETTING YOUR CHILD GO KETO

We have already gone through the potential benefits of the ketogenic diet. But now, I will share with you the medical side of the diet. Since this diet was developed primarily for the treatment of epilepsy, it seems to have a lot of medical applications and advantages. Here are some examples of medical conditions that may benefit from the ketogenic diet:

1. Infantile Spasms

According to the Child Neurology Society and the American Academy of Neurology, the very first line of therapy for this condition is the adrenocorticotropic hormone (ACTH). Infants who suffer from this condition can be given medication to improve their abnormal EEG and halt the infantile spasms completely. Some pediatric neurologists may prescribe specific seizure medications, especially for infants who have tuberous sclerosis. Such medications may work well for the treatment of infantile spasms but sometimes, these don't work. In such cases, doctors may recommend the ketogenic diet to help with the treatment. This is especially helpful when administered early on. Over time, this diet can be more beneficial to children with infantile spasms compared to medications.

2. Epilepsy

Of course, the ketogenic diet is beneficial for children with epilepsy as the diet was originally developed to help with its treatment. Aside from epilepsy, some children may have some types of metabolic disorders that make it difficult for their bodies to break carbs down and utilize these for fuel. For such disorders, the ketogenic diet can also be beneficial. When it comes to the treatment of epilepsy using the keto diet, a child may have to undergo a fast for 1 to 2 days while being medically monitored by their doctor. Fasting is required for the process of ketosis to kick in wherein the child's body will start producing ketones. After the fast, the child will be allowed to eat but this time, the doctor will increase their fat intake gradually for a couple of days. During this time, the doctor will continuously monitor the child to ensure that they don't experience any negative side effects.

If the child's body has successfully adjusted to the increased fat intake without any adverse changes, they can be fed keto shakes before they move on to solid food. Throughout this transition period, the child will be monitored by their doctor, a registered nurse, and even a registered dietician. All of these medical professionals ensure that the diet is helping with the child's therapy and doesn't develop any nutrient deficiencies.

While the child is being treated in the hospital and is being gradually introduced to the ketogenic diet, the child's parents will also be taught how to continue the diet at home. Since the diet will be part of the child's treatment, parents won't just be taught how to encourage the child to follow the diet. Parents should also learn how to check their child's ketone levels to ensure that they are in ketosis. Also, parents would have to learn how to properly go through food labels and labels of other products that may contain carbs like medications, toothpaste, and mouthwash. While you don't have to be this strict if your child is healthy, these are things that you would have to check if your child is following the ketogenic diet for medical reasons.

After the child has followed the ketogenic diet for days and the doctor deems it successful, then the child may be sent home. By this time, the child may be prescribed with fewer medications to see if the diet can be more helpful in reducing the symptoms of their condition. By the time the child is allowed to go home, their parents should already have enough knowledge about the diet so they can continue administering it at home. Also, the child must be brought to the doctor for regular check-ups to monitor their symptoms and metabolism.

3. Seizures

Seizures are the most common—and debilitating—symptom of epilepsy. For children who suffer from severe epilepsy, they can experience hundreds of seizures each day. Of course, this will limit their quality of life severely as it can prevent them from taking part in social and school activities. When a child is given seizure medications that don't seem to work, then the doctor may recommend that the child start the ketogenic diet. This diet can be a possible treatment option when the seizures are disrupting the child's life and medications just aren't working. As with children who suffer from epilepsy, those who experience seizures should also start the keto diet under the close supervision and monitoring of their doctor and a team of medical professionals. For this condition, the type of ketogenic diet to be administered will depend on:

- The age of the child.
- The weight of the child.
- The culture and dietary habits of the child's family.
- The child's recommended macronutrient breakdown.

While the diet can be very beneficial for children who suffer from seizures, it may not work for everyone. Potentially, though, this diet can be helpful for different types of conditions that include seizures such as myoclonic-astatic epilepsy, migrational disorders, Doose syndrome, Dravet syndrome, Rett syndrome, and GLUT-1 deficiency.

4. Autism

The ketogenic diet also has the potential to manage autism and its most common symptoms. Some studies have shown that when children with autism started following intermittent ketogenic diets, **they experienced positive changes in**

their behavior. Specifically, the studies showed that the diet may help reduce the symptoms of the condition, thus, improve the child's quality of life. This, in turn, results in improved behaviors too. Since the children aren't bothered by their symptoms, this reduces their tendency to act out. This is an important advantage so that parents can manage their kids' behaviors more effectively.

5. Attention Deficit Hyperactivity Disorder (ADHD)

The ketogenic diet can also be helpful for ADHD as it can improve the symptoms of this condition too. For children who suffer from ADHD, parents are recommended to increase the child's intake of omega-3 and omega-6 while reducing their carb intake, especially sugar. As you know, both of these dietary recommendations are part of the ketogenic diet, thus, it means that the diet will truly be helpful for children who suffer from this condition.

6. Other medical advantages

Although so many studies have already been conducted on the ketogenic diet, the exact effects (both good and bad) aren't completely understood yet. However, there are plenty of studies and research which have shown how this diet can benefit health in different ways. Here are other medical advantages of the keto diet to look forward to:

- The ketogenic diet may improve the function of brain cells, specifically with how they communicate with each other. This benefit protects the brain by restoring homeostasis. For instance, while a child follows the diet, it may calm the nerve cells that are excessively stimulated or ramp up the nerve cells that aren't stimulated enough.
- During the process of ketosis, the body produces

ketones which, in turn, provide the brain with an alternative source of fuel to keep functioning despite the restriction of carbs from the diet. When the brain is primarily running on ketones, this may lead to a reduction in oxidative stress.

- The ketogenic diet has anti-inflammatory effects which make it highly beneficial in the prevention of chronic diseases.
- The ketogenic diet can also make a positive impact on the gut microbiome. This impact may result in an improvement of the communication between the brain and the gut which, in turn, leads to other beneficial effects, especially for those suffering from epilepsy and autism spectrum disorders.

While all of these health advantages have already been seen in countless patients of different ages, more research is needed to prove these advantages conclusively. Also, there are so many factors to consider when administering the diet, especially to children. Furthermore, the diet doesn't necessarily work for all children. For some children, the ketogenic diet may improve their treatment while for others, the diet might not make any significant impact. Even though this diet is generally beneficial to health, it isn't consistent enough to be considered as the first or most effective option for the treatment of various medical conditions.

When used for the treatment of medical conditions, doctors may only recommend that a child would follow the diet for a specific amount of time. Usually, this would take up to 2 years if the diet has proven to improve the symptoms or the condition of the child. After this time, the doctor may recommend that the child be weaned off the diet gradually. However, there have been cases where children who suffer from medical conditions are allowed to follow the diet for several years. This is especially true for children who suffer from epilepsy.

On the other hand, if your child's doctor observes that the diet isn't doing them any good or if your child finds the diet too restrictive that it is making them miserable, you may have to switch to a different diet. Whenever you make any changes to your child's diet, make sure to do this gradually. Making drastic changes in a short amount of time might affect your child adversely and they might experience the potential side effects. If you are thinking about discontinuing the diet for whatever reason, speak with your child's doctor. This is the best way to ensure your child's safety as you help them transition back to their regular diet.

THE POTENTIAL RISKS AND DISADVANTAGES OF THE KETOGENIC DIET FOR CHILDREN

Lorem The ketogenic diet may offer a lot of benefits but it also comes with its own set of potential risks and disadvantages. For one, this diet can cause a number of side effects even if your child follows it correctly. Some of the most common side effects include:

- Constipation
- Diarrhea
- Dehydration
- Fatigue
- Nausea
- Vomiting

Typically, these mild side effects manifest at the beginning of the diet when your child's body is adjusting to it. But as long as you keep your child well-hydrated and you take things slow, you don't have to worry about these adverse effects as much. However, some parents have noticed irritability and hyperactivity in their children after a few days of following this diet. However, these mild symptoms tend to fade away after some time. Apart from these mild side effects, this diet also comes with potential side effects that are much more severe including:

- bone density loss
- electrolyte imbalances
- increased levels of cholesterol
- higher risk of infections
- kidney stones
- poor growth

All of these side effects might occur if you cannot guide your child to follow the diet correctly. Mainly, your child will be at risk for these side effects if their body thinks that it is starving. Naturally, when you limit your child's carb intake, their body will feel like it is starving although it is only being starved of glucose. So if you also restrict your child's caloric intake, this might cause the emergence of the side effects whether mild or severe. This is why you should take things slow.

There are some cases when the keto diet may harm the concentration and focus of children too. These also happen around the beginning of their keto journey as their bodies are transitioning from using glucose for fuel to using fat for fuel. As their body adjusts to this change, they might experience a drop in their energy levels too.

Most of the side effects fade away after some time. For some of the side effects, they may fade away or even get reversed when you transition your child back to a normal diet. Then there are some side effects that you need to report to your child's doctor so that your child's health can be monitored. Your child's doctor can also provide you with an explanation of why these side effects have emerged and what you can do to get rid of them.

While you can reduce the risk or prevent the potential side effects of the ketogenic diet, there is one important risk that you should focus on: nutrient deficiency. Since the keto diet involves restricting carbs and sugar, this means that you will be eliminating several types of food from their diet. When you do this, your child might end up developing nutrient deficiencies, especially if the diet isn't followed correctly. Nutrient deficiencies develop when children don't get enough of a certain vitamin, mineral or macronutrient from the food they eat. Although this won't happen right away, children may develop these deficiencies over time if their diets are always insufficient in terms of these essential nutrients.

Nutrient deficiencies can be very dangerous as they might interfere with the normal growth and development of your child. When adults follow the keto diet, it's a lot easier to avoid this issue. But for children, it's more difficult to avoid and manage when they have already developed this condition. If you want to prevent your child from developing any kind of nutrient deficiency, then it's best to ask help from your child's doctor. Your child's doctor can conduct the required tests on your child to check for any deficiencies. For this issue, it's better if your child's doctor can diagnose it early on. Then your child's doctor can give you recommendations on how to improve their diet to overcome the deficiencies or even prescribe supplements for your child to take.

Another potential risk that you have to be aware of when it comes to the keto diet also happens to be one of the benefits: weight loss. If your child already has a healthy weight, this is one benefit that you don't have to aim for when you encourage your child to go keto. To avoid this, you don't have to restrict their carb intake right away. For instance, children who are following a regular diet should normally eat 130g of carbs each day but when they follow keto, this amount should be drastically reduced to a mere 20g to 30g per day. If you don't want your child to lose weight drastically on the diet, then you don't have to reduce their carb intake right away. Instead, focus on giving your child healthier types of carbs. In doing this, you are still promoting healthy habits without having to risk your child's healthy weight.

As you can see, the keto diet comes with a few downsides you should be aware of. Now that you know them, you can observe your child more carefully while you guide them through the diet. To help you out even more, here are a few final tips to consider in terms of risks and side effects of the keto diet:

- The ketogenic diet will only work effectively if you follow it correctly. Even then, it can still cause some side effects or in some cases, it might not even benefit your child.
- As you have learned, this restrictive diet comes with some potentially serious side effects. If you want to avoid these, communicate openly with your child's doctor so that your child can be monitored carefully, especially during the transition phase.
- For a lot of people, the ketogenic diet isn't considered a balanced, healthy eating plan for the long term. If

you want your child to follow this diet for the foreseeable future, make sure to learn everything that you can about it so that you can keep your child safe. Also, if you discover that the diet isn't affecting your child positively anymore, consider shifting them back to a regular diet but this time, focus more on whole, healthy foods.

- The ketogenic diet isn't recommended for children who suffer from fatty acid oxidation defects and other types of metabolic disorders. If your child suffers from such a condition, consult with their doctor first. If your child's doctor says that keto isn't recommended, follow their advice.

When it comes to the risks and downsides of the ketogenic diet, being aware of these isn't enough. Always prioritize your child's health and safety, otherwise, there would be no point in encouraging your child to go keto. Remember that your main purpose for letting them follow the diet is to encourage healthier eating habits. But if the diet isn't right for your child, it would be better to teach them these healthy habits in other ways. You may also consider other types of diets that are less restrictive if these will benefit your child more.

4

MEAL PREPS FOR THE KETOGENIC DIET FOR CHILDREN

Fig. 5: Meal Prep. Unsplash, by S'well, 2019, https://unsplash.com/photos/CJdZ800-Fbs/ Copyright 2019 by S'well/Unsplash.

Meal preps are an important part of the ketogenic diet, especially for children. For adults, it's much easier to follow keto even when you're not at home because you know how to find keto-friendly meals and snacks while at work, while traveling, and while eating out with other people. But for kids, they would typically eat the same things as their friends, especially while at school. Therefore, it's your responsibility to prepare your child's meals and snacks from home so that they always have keto-friendly food to eat during breaks or whenever they get hungry.

Meal prep or meal planning involves creating a weekly plan for the meals you will be feeding your child from the start to the end of each day. For instance, you would create a plan that looks like this:

- Monday: Breakfast, Lunch, Snacks, Dinner

- Tuesday: Breakfast, Lunch, Snacks, Dinner
- Wednesday: Breakfast, Lunch, Snacks, Dinner
- ... and so on.

Before you make your plan, check your refrigerator for any leftovers. If you have any, you can include them on the first days of your plan. After you make your meal plan, check your pantry for any leftover ingredients that you can use to cook your planned meals. Then you would create a shopping list that includes all of the other ingredients you need. Ideally, you would set aside one day for planning and shopping for ingredients and another day for preparing the ingredients and cooking your child's meals. For the rest of the days, all you have to do is serve those meals to your child!

Although meal prep may take some getting used to, it will make your life simpler and easier. Once you get the hang of this process, you won't have to worry about what to feed your child throughout the week. You can even involve your child in the planning process so that they look forward to the meals you have prepared. If you are also following the keto diet, then meal prep becomes much easier since you would be cooking the same meals for yourself, your kids, and maybe even your family. In such a case, just increase the servings of the recipes you cook then divide the dishes according to the number of your family members. Meal prep is a very flexible process that can even help make the diet more fun for you and your child to follow.

Another thing you must do before you start meal prepping is to clear your kitchen and pantry of all non-keto foods and ingredients. That way, you will be left only with ingredients and foods that are suitable for the diet that you can use for your meal preps. Remember to give these food items away instead of just throwing them out to avoid food waste. Then if you will go shopping, here are some basics to look out for in food shops:

Dairy

- butter (salted and unsalted)
- cream cheese
- plain yogurt

Oils and spices

- avocado oil
- cinnamon
- coconut oil
- garlic powder
- ginger
- pepper
- salt
- sesame oil
- sesame seeds

Pantry supplies

- almond butter
- almond flour
- chicken broth
- cocoa powder
- coconut cream
- monk fruit extract
- soy sauce
- vanilla extract

Produce

- avocado
- cherry tomatoes
- garlic
- green cabbage
- green onions
- leaf or Romaine lettuce
- lime
- mushrooms
- red bell pepper
- spinach
- white onion

Proteins

- bacon
- breakfast sausages
- chicken breasts
- eggs
- ground beef

These are some examples of the most common food items you can keep in your pantry for your meal preps. As you will soon come to realize, cooking on keto is quite easy as long as you are familiar with the foods that are allowed on keto and the foods that you should avoid. Then you can mix and match all of these ingredients to create scrumptious dishes that your child will surely love.

While some people feel intimidated at the mere thought of meal prepping, I personally recommend it because it's efficient and it simplifies things. Whenever I include my daughters in this process, we have a lot of fun planning, shopping, prepping, and cooking. Of course, we also have a lot of fun eating the meals we prepare together! To help start you off, here are some of the most basic steps involved in meal prep:

Set a schedule for planning your meals

Planning your meals for the week takes practice. The first few times you do this, you might take a long time to accomplish the task, especially if you have to rely on recipes that aren't familiar to you. But if you keep doing this every week, you'll surely get the hang of it. You can even download meal prep templates online and print these out so all you have to do is write down the meals. The important thing is to set aside time to make your meal plans so you can start shopping for the ingredients you need.

Create your own recipe book for meal preps

Recipes are an important part of meal prep. In this eBook, you will learn 25 new recipes to start your brand-new keto cookbook. Use a clear book to keep all of your printed recipes and you can even save copies on your computer. After you practice making these dishes, you can go online and look for more. Whenever you find a new recipe that works for your child and your family, add it to your recipe book. Then keep this book by your side when you're planning meals so that you can use it as a reference, especially when you're having a hard time thinking of what to prepare for your child.

Involve your child in the process

Finally, since you will mainly be focusing on meals for your child, involve them in the process as much as possible. Remember that this is an effective way to motivate your child to keep following the diet. Sit down together to plan your meals for the week, take your child with you when you go shopping for ingredients, and allow your child to help you out with cooking some of the dishes. Keep inviting your child to join you but if they aren't interested, that's okay. Don't force them into taking part in your meal prep activities as they might see this as a chore instead of something fun to do.

THE BASIC INGREDIENTS YOU NEED FOR COOKING ON KETO FOR CHILDREN

If you want your child to get the most out of the ketogenic diet, then it's best to focus on whole foods instead of processed food products even if the labels state that they are keto-friendly. While you can allow your child to eat these processed keto-friendly products, it's still healthier to feed them whole foods more often. For this, think of healthy fats, high-quality protein, and nutrient-dense carbs. Some examples of whole foods that children enjoy are:

- avocado
- bacon
- berries
- boiled eggs
- cheese
- chicken
- low-carb veggies
- yogurt

While these foods can already be served on their own, you can also start creating a wide range of dishes and snacks for your child to thrive on the diet. When looking for recipes to make for your child, keep the following considerations in mind:

- Kids must eat **healthy fats** that contain essential fatty acids. These fats keep kids feeling full for longer periods while supplying fat-soluble vitamins including vitamin A, vitamin D, vitamin E, and vitamin K.

- Kids must eat **high-quality protein** to support their growth and development.
- Kids must eat **nutrient-dense carbs** to ensure the optimal functioning of their heart, brain, digestive, immune, and nervous systems. While you should reduce the number of carbs they eat, focusing on healthy, nutrient-dense carbs will help prevent the potential side effects of the diet.
- Kids must eat **low-starch vegetables** as these will provide them with antioxidants, fiber, minerals, vitamins, and other nutrients to make them grow big and strong.
- Kids must also eat **low-starch fruits** as these contain essential nutrients too. Of course, since most fruits are high in starch and sugar, you should reduce their consumption of these healthy foods too. Also, opt for fresh fruits instead of dried fruits or fruit juices as these typically contain added sugars.

Make sure to plan your child's meals while keeping all of these points in mind. When cooking on keto, there are certain ingredients that you will be using frequently whether you are whipping up savory recipes, sweet desserts or even snacks. Stock your pantry with these ingredients to make it easier for you to plan meals and even to cook recipes that aren't included in your plan for times when your child requests for specific meals or snacks. While following the ketogenic diet, here are some of the most basic ingredients you may need:

1. Almond Flour

This type of flour is low in carbs but it will add fiber, protein, and a unique taste to your dishes. You can use almond flour for making muffins, cookies, pancakes, and even hearty crusts. You can also use almond flour to replace breadcrumbs when you're making fried foods. This type of flour is available in most supermarkets and health food shops. But you can also make your own almond flour at home by grinding raw almonds finely in a food processor.

2. Eggs

Eggs are rich in protein, healthy fats, and vitamin D. They also contain B vitamins that can promote sleep and give your mood a boost. The great thing about eggs is that you can cook them in different ways and use them in a wide range of recipes too. When buying eggs, opt for the free-range, organic variety, especially if you plan to feed them to kids.

3. Ghee

Ghee is flavorful, concentrated, and it is made from the milk solids and milk proteins taken from butter. It contains high amounts of healthy fats and it offers a number of health benefits as it supports digestion, reduces the risk of developing heart disease, and it can even help your child maintain a healthy weight. You can use ghee for roasting, sautéing, and as a substitute for oil and butter in different recipes. If you want to make it more flavorful, you can infuse ghee with spices or herbs like garlic, ginger, curry powder, parsley or chives.

4. Bone Broth

Bone broth is a staple on the ketogenic diet as you can serve it on its own, as a side dish or even mixed in other dishes.

This filling soup is rich in nutrients and it offers benefits to joint health, digestion, and it even has anti-inflammatory properties. Bone broth also contains essential minerals that support the nervous system and the health of the bones. You can cook large batches of bone broth then store it in your refrigerator. Use bone broth in stews, risotto, soups, for cooking grains or one-pot meals, and more. While you can buy bone broth from food shops, it's better to make your own bone broth at home using roasted bones or fresh bones you have bought from the butcher. To add nutrition and flavor to your bone broth, add chopped vegetables to it too.

5. Cacao Powder

If your child loves chocolate then you should definitely have this ingredient in your pantry. Raw cacao powder is rich in magnesium, antioxidants, and iron. It even contains anandamide, a type of neurotransmitter that promotes feelings of bliss and joy. Use cacao powder in smoothies, hot chocolate, desserts, spreads, and pastries. Whenever you want to give something a chocolate flavor, add cacao powder to the mix.

6. Coconut Flour

Just like almond flour, you can use coconut flour as a substitute for carb-rich flour varieties. This type of flour is rich in fiber and protein making it a filling, nutrient-dense ingredient for your keto dishes. Coconut flour is gluten-free and it tends to soak up liquids. This makes it suitable for making waffles, cookies, pancakes, and even as a breading for fish and meat. You can also use coconut flour for making fat bombs, one of the best types of snacks for the keto diet.

7. Coconut Oil

This type of oil has a tropical flavor with a slight hint of sweetness. It has antibacterial, anti-fungal, and anti-viral properties. Furthermore, it has medium-chain fatty acids that are easy for the body to break down, process, and utilize for energy. Coconut oil is great for baking, cooking, and even to add fat to smoothies. When it comes to commercial coconut oil products, some have stronger flavors than others, therefore, you may want to try out different products to find one that your child will like. Also, it's best to opt for unrefined, organic coconut oil as this is much healthier.

8. Olive Oil

Among all the different types of oil available for cooking, olive oil is probably the most popular. This oil is famous for being heart-healthy and it also offers anti-inflammatory and antioxidant properties. Use this oil for making salad dressings, dips, for sautéing, for making sauces, and even for frying. If possible, opt for unrefined, cold-pressure olive oil as this is much healthier. This variation comes in dark-colored glass bottles.

These are some of the most common ingredients to keep in your kitchen or pantry so you will always be ready to whip up keto-friendly dishes. As you practice cooking, you will discover more and more ingredients to use and you can keep these in your pantry along with the basics.

MEAL PREP TIPS FOR MOMS

Now that you understand what meal prep involves and you have an idea of the basic ingredients to keep in your pantry, you're just about ready to start this helpful process. Although you don't have to learn meal prep as part of the ketogenic diet, this can be extremely helpful, especially if you also have work or other responsibilities to deal with. Often, parents aren't able to encourage their children to stick with the diet because they don't have the time to prepare homemade meals. So they resort to giving their kids money for their school lunches.

Unfortunately, most schools don't offer keto-friendly fare or any other types of specialty foods for students who follow different types of diets. If your child eats regular, high-carb food in school, they cannot follow the keto diet correctly. This is where meal prep comes in. Through meal prep, you will prepare all of your child's meals for a whole week so they will be ready to eat at any time of the day. You can also send the meals you have prepped with your child to school so they can continue following keto even when you're not around. Here are a few stellar meal prep tips to help you out:

1. Always search for new recipes

Whenever you have free time, use this to search for new recipes online or from other resources. The recipes you will be learning in the next few chapters will make you really popular with your child but let's face it, you can't keep feeding them the same thing over and over again. So you must keep searching for new recipes to entice your child. Learning how to cook new dishes also hones your kitchen skills which, in turn, you can teach your child.

2. Make things more interesting by assigning themes to your child's meals

The minute you assign themes to your meals, you are also adding fun to your child's diet. For instance, you can have Pizza Mondays (yes, you can make keto-friendly pizza), Noodle Saturdays or even Dessert days. You can also base your themes on the shows your child loves watching. As you are planning your child's meals for the week, try to assign a theme to one day. If you want the theme to run throughout the day, then you can assign this to a weekday when your child doesn't have to go to school. You can also set the theme day on weekdays as long as you make sure that the meals you prepare all fit into the theme. This might even make your child happier as they can show off their themed meals at school.

3. Change or remove meals from your plan before finalizing it

Just like any other plan, your meal plan may have to go through some changes before finalization. Typically, the changes would be required if you are keeping track of your child's caloric intake each day. Since the ketogenic diet involves specific macronutrient percentages, you may choose to follow these. You can also make changes to your meal plan if you discover that one day consists of heavy meals from breakfast to dinner or another day only consists of light meals. Make sure that all of the daily meal plans are well-balanced so your child doesn't go hungry or doesn't feel full throughout the day.

4. Bring a list with you when you go shopping

After creating your plan, take an inventory of the ingredients you have in your stocks. Then make a separate list of ingredients that you need to cook all the meals in your plan. Make sure to bring the list you made when you go shopping so you can buy everything you need. It's probably a good idea to include some back-up recipes in your plan too. That way, you can buy the ingredients of these recipes if some of the ingredients for your original plans aren't available in the supermarket. The more flexible you are with your meal preps, the easier you will learn this process.

5. Prepare your child's meals in advance

After purchasing everything you need for the meals you have planned for the week, it's time to start cooking. Set a separate schedule for cooking all of the meals in your plan. You may opt to plan, shop, and cook in one day but this might tire you out. Also, you might not be able to do anything else if you try to do all of these things in one day. Instead, it's better to plan and shop on one day then prep and cook the next. That way, you can focus on each task better. Also, if you will involve your child in the different steps of the meal prep process, you will need more time to finish everything.

6. Store the meals you've prepared properly

Finally, after you have cooked everything, you need to store the meals properly to avoid spoilage. As you finish cooking each dish, transfer it into an airtight container (or several airtight containers) then leave it on the countertop or table to cool down completely. Once cooled, store the dishes inside the refrigerator until you're ready to serve them to your child. When planning your meals, start with the dishes that tend to spoil easily. That way, you don't end up with spoiled dishes that you have spent a lot of time and money on.

Meal prep doesn't have to be a difficult task. As long as you plan for it and keep practicing it, you will be on your way towards becoming a meal prep master!

5

EASY-TO-MAKE SAVORY KETO SNACK RECIPES

Although everything you have learned may seem easy enough, it's best not to be too strict when letting your children follow the ketogenic diet. For instance, if your children are really craving cookies, you may consider

Fig. 6: Almonds. Pixabay, by Free-Photos, 2015,
https://pixabay.com/photos/almonds-food-nuts-healthy-diet-768649/
Copyright 2015 by Free-Photos/Pixabay.

giving in to this request. Of course, the older your children are, the easier it would be to explain the diet to them along with all of its benefits. On the other hand, if you start your children young, they won't get used to eating carb-rich or sugary foods which means that they won't end up craving such foods. It's all about learning how to remain flexible while encouraging your children to follow this restrictive and specialized diet.

Whether you plan to allow your children to have non-keto treats once in a while or not, you can make things easier for yourself by learning how to make keto snacks. Children are used to eating throughout the day and you can provide them with healthy snacks that they will surely love by learning how to make them. In this chapter (and the next one), you will be learning how to make simple, tasty, and ket0-friendly snacks to keep your children full, satisfied, and happy. First, let's go through some savory snacks that you will also enjoy eating with your children.

LITTLE PIGS IN A BLANKET

Lorem Most kids love eating hot dogs. While this isn't the healthiest of food options, there is still something about hot dogs that seem to appeal to children all over the world. If you and your children love hot dogs, then you will love these little pigs in a blanket. Obviously, this is a keto- and child-friendly version of the traditional pigs in a blanket treat that is usually served at parties. This tasty dish is easy to make and it tastes just like the real thing. Plus, you can let your children join you in preparing these little pigs in a blanket to make the whole experience more fun for them.

Time: 30 minutes

Serving Size: 4 servings

Ingredients:

- ¼ tsp baking powder
- ¼ tsp garlic powder
- ½ tsp sesame seeds
- ½ tsp salt
- ½ cup of mozzarella cheese (shredded)
- ¾ cup of almond flour
- 1 large egg
- 4 medium-sized hot dogs (you can also use 12 cocktail hot dogs)

Directions:

- Cut each of the hot dogs into 3 pieces of roughly the same size then set them aside.
- In a microwave-safe bowl, add the mozzarella cheese, place it in the microwave, and melt it.
- Add the egg and the almond flour then mix until well-combined.
- Add the garlic powder, salt, and baking powder then continue mixing until well-combined to create your dough.
- Divide the dough into 12 pieces of roughly the same size and roll the pieces of dough into balls.
- Use your hand or a rolling pin to flatten the dough balls into oval shapes.
- Place the dough ovals on a baking sheet lined with parchment paper.
- Place each of the cut-up hot dog pieces into the dough ovals then wrap them up as you would a child in a blanket.
- Sprinkle each of the little pigs in a blanket with sesame seeds. Lightly press the sesame seeds into the dough so they don't fall off.
- Place the baking sheet in the oven at 350°F and bake the little pigs in a blanket for about 17 to 20 minutes.
- Once cooked, take the baking sheet out of the oven and allow the little pigs in a blanket to cool down before serving.
- You can serve these on their own or with a keto-friendly dipping sauce.

CHEESY CAULI-TOTS

Whipping up keto-friendly snacks for children is all about being creative in the kitchen. You can still make classic favorites by changing the ingredients to make them keto-friendly. With this recipe, you

Fig. 8: Cauli-Tots. Unsplash, by Filiz Elaerts, 2020. https://unsplash.com/photos/olnWmfVxEnw/ Copyright 2020 by Filiz Elaerts/Unsplash.

will be making your own tater tots—a very popular snack for children—but this time, you will change the main ingredient into something that fits into the ketogenic diet. While children love potatoes, cauliflower is an excellent substitute as it's just as tasty and filling for different dishes. For this recipe, adding cheese to the mix makes it even better!

Time: 30 minutes

Serving Size: 20 to 24 cauli-tots depending on the size

Ingredients:

- ½ tsp mustard (ground)
- 1 tsp salt
- ¼ cup of cornmeal
- 1 cup of old cheddar cheese (shredded, you can also use any other cheese of your choice)
- 3 cups of cauliflower (raw, shredded)
- 1 large egg
- butter

Directions:

- Preheat your oven to 400°F and place a mini muffin tin that you have greased with butter.

- If you haven't shredded the cauliflower yet, use a grater or food processor to do this.
- After shredding, transfer the shredded cauliflower into a clean dish towel.
- Wrap the shredded cauliflower with the dish towel then squeeze it hard to remove the excess water.
- In a bowl, add the shredded cauliflower along with the rest of the ingredients. Use a fork to mix everything together until well-combined.
- Take the preheated mini muffin tin out of the oven.
- Use a spoon to scoop the cauli-tots mixture into the mini muffin tins. Press down gently to flatten.
- If you don't have a mini muffin tin, you can use a baking sheet lined with parchment to place your cauli-tots. Before placing them on the baking sheet, shape them into cauli-tots using your hands.
- Place the mini muffin tin in the oven and bake the cauli-tots for about 18 to 20 minutes until they are golden-brown.
- Once cooked, take the mini muffin tin out of the oven and allow the cheesy cauli-tots to cool down slightly before serving.
- You can serve these on their own or with a keto-friendly dipping sauce.

PULL-APART KETO PIZZA BREAD

Yes, your children can still have pizza even while following the ketogenic diet. This recipe is tasty, cheesy, and oh-so-fun to eat! Think about it: pizza that you can share as a family by pulling apart the pieces before eating it. You can whip up this fun dish with your kids and serve it as a savory snack or a light dinner. It's also super fun to eat when you have a game or movie night with the whole family. This is a great dish to serve at parties too!

Time: 35 minutes

Serving Size: 16 servings

Ingredients:

- 1 tsp rosemary seasoning
- 1 tbsp baking powder
- ¼ cup of cream cheese
- ½ cup of mild cheddar cheese (shredded)
- ½ cup of mini pepperoni slices
- ½ cup of Parmesan cheese (grated)
- 1 ½ cups of almond flour
- 2 ½ cups of mozzarella cheese (shredded)
- 3 medium-sized eggs (beaten)
- jalapeño slices (optional)
- cooking spray

Directions:

- In a bowl, add the baking powder and almond flour then mix until fully combined. Set aside.
- In a microwave-safe bowl, combine the cream cheese and mozzarella cheese, place it in the microwave and melt it. Mix well to combine.
- Add the melted cheeses to the flour mixture along with the eggs.
- Mix the ingredients well until you form a dough. Use your hands to knead the dough until you form a ball. Take note that this dough will be quite sticky so you may want to do this on a silicone mat if you have one. Otherwise, you can just sprinkle almond flour

on the surface where you will knead the dough so it doesn't stick too much.

- After you have mixed all of the ingredients together fully and your dough ball has come together, sprinkle some parmesan cheese on top of it. This makes the dough ball less sticky as you start forming it. You can sprinkle parmesan cheese all over too.

- Divide the dough into two and set half aside. For the other half, continue dividing it until you have 16 pieces of dough that are roughly the same size. These will be the pull-apart pieces.

- In a shallow dish, combine the parmesan cheese with rosemary seasoning and mix well.

- Roll the pieces of dough into balls then coat each of the dough balls with the seasoned parmesan cheese.

- Roll the other half of the dough into a ball and coat it with the seasoned parmesan cheese too.

- Grease a bundt pan with cooking spray and place the large dough ball in the middle. Gently press down on it to flatten slightly.

- Stick the smaller dough balls all around the large dough ball to form the pull-apart pizza bread.

- Top it off with a layer of mild cheddar cheese, slices of mini pepperoni, and jalapeño if using. You can also add your own toppings as long as they are keto-friendly.

- Place the bundt pan in the oven at 350°F and bake the pull-apart pizza bread for about 25 minutes. You can adjust the cooking time based on the size and thickness of your pizza bread.

- Once cooked, take the bundt pan out of the oven and allow the pull-apart pizza bread to cool slightly before serving.

COLORFUL VEGGIE EGG CUPS

Have you ever tried eating egg cups before? Egg cups are so easy to make and they make eggs a lot more interesting to eat. When you add veggies to them, you will find it easier to convince your children to eat their veggies. The best part about this recipe is that it's completely customizable. As long as you follow the basic steps, you can make different versions of egg cups using different ingredients. You can even make a game out of it where you layout different ingredients and ask your children to add their own. Just make sure that the ingredients you offer are all healthy and keto-friendly.

Time: 25 minutes

Serving Size: 12 servings

Ingredients:

- ⅓ cup of brie cheese (chopped)
- ½ cup of milk
- 1 ½ cups of spinach (chopped)
- 1 red bell pepper (seeds removed, chopped)
- 6 large eggs
- cooking spray
- salt

Directions:

- Preheat your oven to 350°F and grease a muffin tray with cooking spray
- In a bowl, combine the eggs and milk then beat together thoroughly.
- Add all the other ingredients to the bowl and

continue mixing until everything is well-incorporated.

- Gently pour the egg cup mixture into the muffin tray. Try to divide the mixture equally so that all of the egg cups cook at the same time.
- Place the muffin tray in the oven and cook the egg cups for about 18 to 20 minutes until completely set.
- Once cooked, take the muffin tray out of the oven and allow the egg cups to cool before serving. You can serve these egg cups warm or allow them to cool down completely and have your kids enjoy them cold.

CHEESE AND BROCCOLI NUGGETS

This final recipe rounds off our selection of savory snack options and it's another popular choice. It's crunchy, filling, savory, and healthy too. If your children aren't fans of broccoli, they might change their minds once you serve these nuggets to them. This simple recipe only requires a few ingredients and you can easily make it with your children. You can serve it as a snack or as a side dish for when you're preparing your children's school lunches. Either way, this is another winning dish for a kid-friendly ketogenic diet.

Time: 25 minutes

Serving Size: 4 servings

Ingredients:

- ¼ cup of almond flour
- 1 cup of Monterey Jack cheese (shredded)
- 2 cups of broccoli florets (frozen or fresh, cooked until soft)

- 2 eggs (whites only)
- cooking spray
- salt

Directions:

- Preheat your oven to 350°F and grease a cookie sheet with cooking spray.
- In a bowl, add the cooked broccoli florets then break them up using a potato masher.
- Add all of the other ingredients to the bowl then mix until everything is well-incorporated.
- Use a spoon or your hand to take small portions of the mixture and shape them into nuggets then place the nuggets on the greased cookie sheet. Try to make nuggets that are roughly the same size so that they cook at the same time.
- Place the cookie sheet in the oven and bake the nuggets for about 20 minutes until golden brown and firm. The cooking time will depend on the size of your nuggets.
- Once cooked, take the cookie sheet out of the oven and allow to cool slightly before serving.
- You can serve these on their own or with a keto-friendly dipping sauce.

6

EASY-TO-MAKE SWEET KETO SNACK RECIPES

Fig. 8: Blackberries. Pixabay, by congerdesign, 2017,
https://pixabay.com/photos/blueberries-dessert-fruit-fruits-2278921/
Copyright 2017 by congerdesign/Pixabay.

As a parent, trying to get your children to eat healthily can be a challenge, especially if you have a job to deal with too. Even more so when you're trying to get your children to follow a restrictive diet such as keto. Fortunately, going keto now isn't as difficult as it was in the past. Because of the diet's popularity, there are now so many dishes you can whip up to ensure that your children follow the diet without feeling like you are restricting them severely.

For a lot of kids, sweet treats are very appealing. But as you know, sugar isn't allowed on keto. However, this doesn't mean that you have to completely remove sweets from your kids' diet. The key here is to use keto-approved sweeteners to make easy and tasty sweet snacks that are 100% keto-friendly. Learning how to make these sweet snacks will make the ketogenic diet easier to follow so your kids won't feel like they're struggling with it. Try practicing with these simple recipes and later, you can start making more complex ones to keep your kids happy and interested. These recipes are so easy and tasty that you can share them with the whole family!

STEVIA-SWEETENED MERINGUE COOKIES

Meringue is a classic and we all love how light and crunchy it is. Now think about this lovely texture but this time, in the form of keto-friendly cookies. These tasty meringue cookies are sweetened with stevia, a keto-approved sweetener. They are also made with cream of tartar and egg whites making them the perfect low-carb snack. These cookies are light, airy, and have just the right amount of sweetness to satisfy your kids' sweet tooth without breaking their keto diet.

Time: 2 hours, 10 minutes

Serving Size: 40 to 48 cookies depending on the size

Ingredients:

- ¾ tsp cream of tartar
- ¾ tsp stevia drops
- 5 medium-sized eggs (whites only)

Directions:

- Preheat your oven to 215°F.
- Line a large cookie sheet with parchment paper. You may also use two small cookie sheets depending on the size of your oven.
- In a bowl, combine the egg whites and cream of tartar then beat until you start forming soft peaks with the mixture.

- Continue beating the mixture while adding the stevia drops. You know that the mixture is ready when you start forming stiff peaks.
- Use a spoon to transfer the mixture to the cookie sheet. The size of the meringue cookies will depend on the size of your spoon or the size of the portions you spoon onto the cookie sheet.
- Place the cookie sheet in the oven and bake the meringue cookies for about 2 hours until they start browning.
- Once cooked, turn the oven off. You can leave the cookie sheet in the oven while still warm until they reach the color you desire.
- Take the cookie sheet out of the oven and allow the meringue cookies to cool down completely before serving.

PROTEIN-PACKED PEANUT BUTTER BALLS

These sweet little treats are rich in healthy fat and protein making them perfect for the ketogenic diet. Since peanut butter is another classic favorite of kids, your little ones will surely enjoy munching on these peanut butter balls. You can give them to your kids as a snack or a dessert to add to their fat and protein intake of the day. The best part is, these peanut butter balls are so easy to make! After making a whole batch, store them in an airtight container to make them readily available to your kids whenever they get a craving for something sweet.

Time: 30 minutes

Serving Size: 20 to 24 balls depending on the size

Ingredients:

- 2 tsp vanilla extract
- ½ protein powder (vanilla, kid-friendly)
- ½ cup erythritol (powdered)
- 1 cup of peanut butter (salted, thick and creamy)
- ½ cup of peanuts (optional, chopped)

Directions:

- In a food processor, add the vanilla extract, protein powder, erythritol, and peanut butter.
- Pulse until you get a mixture with a smooth and even texture. If you need to, scrape down the sides using a spatula.
- You know that the mixture is done when it is very dense and you can press it together. If your mixture is too thin, you may add protein powder or erythritol to it. Add little by little until you get the right texture.
- If using, you stir in the peanuts using a spatula. You can also pulse the peanuts into the mixture but not for too long as this will change the mixture's consistency.
- Transfer the mixture to a bowl and place it in the refrigerator for about 20 minutes to firm up. This is an optional step that also makes the mixture less sticky to handle.
- Wash your hands with cold water before preparing the peanut butter balls.
- Use a spoon to take portions of the mixture then shape the portions into balls using your hands.
- Place the peanut butter balls on a plate after forming them.
- Place the plate in the refrigerator to chill the peanut butter balls until you're ready to serve them to your kids.

CHOCOLATE CHIP MUFFINS

Muffins are a very popular snack option, especially for kids. This is a classic chocolate chip muffin recipe made with keto-friendly ingredients. These muffins are tender, sweet, healthy, and when freshly-baked, your kids will surely keep coming back for more. These muffins also happen to be gluten-free, dairy-free, and oh-so-satisfying. They're the perfect snack to tide your kids over until dinnertime.

Fig. 9: Muffins. Unsplash, by Dessy Dimcheva, 2019, https://unsplash.com/photos/5Q NMQVWIiuU/ Copyright 2019 by Dessa Dimcheva/Unsplash.

Time: 25 minutes

Serving Size: 12 muffins

Ingredients:

- ¼ tsp salt
- ½ tsp baking soda
- 1 tsp vanilla extract
- ¼ cup of avocado oil (melted, cooled, you can also use coconut oil)
- ¼ cup of maple syrup (sugar-free)
- ½ cup of chocolate chips (sugar-free, dairy-free, and gluten-free)
- 2 cups of almond flour (blanched)
- 3 large eggs

Directions:

- Preheat your oven to 350°F then line a muffin pan with paper liners, and set aside.
- In a bowl, combine the baking soda, almond flour, and salt then whisk everything together until well-combined.
- Add the eggs, vanilla extract, maple syrup, and avocado oil then continue mixing until all of the ingredients are well-incorporated.
- Stir the chocolate chips into the mixture.
- Use a spoon to transfer the batter into the muffin pan evenly. Make sure that each paper liner contains roughly the same amount of batter so that all the muffins cook at the same time.
- Place the muffin pan in the oven and bake the muffins for about 20 minutes until they are cooked in the center.
- Once cooked, take the muffin pan out of the oven and allow the muffins to cool for up to 10 minutes before serving.
- If you have any leftover muffins, place them in an airtight container and store at room temperature.

COOKIE FAT BOMBS

Fat bombs are essential to the keto diet as they contain high quantities of healthy fats in bite-sized pieces. There are so many different variations of fat bombs but since we are focused on kid-friendly recipes, these cookie fat bombs are a perfect choice. Fat bombs are especially beneficial in the afternoon when your children are tired and hungry for sweet snacks. These fat bombs contain the healthy fats your children need to run, play, and just be kids. Besides, kids love Oreos, right?

Time: 40 minutes

Serving Size: 16 to 20 fat bombs

Ingredients:

- ¼ tsp salt
- 2 tsp vanilla extract
- 10 tsp monk fruit sweetener (divided in half)
- 4 tbsp cocoa powder
- 8 tbsp coconut oil (melted)
- 1 cup of heavy cream
- 2 cups of almond flour
- 2 cans of coconut milk (full-fat, chilled, separated)
- cooking spray

Directions:

- One day before making the fat bombs, it's recommended to place the cans of coconut milk in the refrigerator. This separates the coconut cream from the water.
- The next day, take the cans of coconut milk out of the refrigerator and skim the cream out using a spoon. You may set the coconut water aside for another recipe.
- In a frying pan, add the almond flour over medium heat and stir constantly for about 2 minutes to toast. Don't leave the flour to cook on its own so it doesn't burn or become too brown.
- In a bowl, combine the toasted almond flour, cocoa powder, coconut oil, salt, and half of the sweetener then stir until well-combined. You know it's done when you have a moist crumb mixture. Set aside.
- In a saucepan, combine the heavy cream, coconut

cream. the other half of the sweetener, and vanilla extract over medium-high heat.

- Whisk the mixture until the sweetener dissolves completely, take the saucepan off the heat, and allow the mixture to cool down.
- Use a muffin pan to mold the cookie fat bombs. Grease the muffin pan lightly with cooking spray to make it easier to take the cookie fat bombs out later on.
- Start by placing about half a teaspoon of cookie crumb mixture into the muffin pan and press down to compact the mixture.
- Spoon around 2 teaspoons of the cream filling into the muffin pan molds leaving about a quarter-inch of space from the top.
- Place the muffin pan in the refrigerator and chill the fat cookie fat bombs for at least 30 minutes.
- Take the muffin pan out of the refrigerator then top each cookie fat bomb off with another half teaspoon of the cookie crumb mixture. Press down to compact the mixture once again.
- Place the muffin pan back into the refrigerator and chill for another 30 minutes before removing the fat bombs from the muffin pan.
- Once removed, transfer the fat bombs to an airtight container to store and make them readily available for snacking.

APPLE AND CINNAMON DONUT BITES

Who doesn't love donuts? And when they come in bite-sized pieces, they become even more exciting and fun to eat. This final recipe in our chapter of sweet snacks will help you learn how to make donut bites with a lovely apple cinnamon flavor. Your kids will surely enjoy these donut bites as a snack or even an occasional breakfast. They're easy to make and the cinnamon coating makes these tiny pastries extra donutty.

Time: 25 minutes

Serving Size: 10 to 12 donut bites depending on the size

Ingredients for the donuts:

- ¼ tsp cinnamon (ground)
- ¼ tsp salt
- 1 tsp apple extract
- 1 tsp baking powder
- 2 tsp apple cider vinegar
- 2 tbsp butter (unsalted, melted)
- 2 tbsp protein powder (kid-friendly)
- 2 tbsp water
- ½ cup of erythritol (granulated)
- 1 cup of almond flour
- 1 medium-sized egg

Ingredients for the cinnamon coating:

- 1 tsp cinnamon (ground)
- 2 tbsp butter (unsalted, melted)
- 2 tbsp keto-friendly sweetener of your choice (powdered)

Directions:

- Preheat your oven to 325°F and grease a muffin pan with cooking spray.
- In a bowl, combine the almond flour, erythritol,

baking powder, protein powder, salt, and cinnamon then mix well.

- Add the water, butter, apple extract, egg, and apple cider vinegar while whisking the mixture.
- Use a spoon to transfer the donut batter into the greased muffin pan. Try to make sure that each muffin pan has equal amounts of batter so they all cook at the same time.
- Place the muffin pan in the oven and bake the donut bites for about 15 to 20 minutes.
- Once cooked, take the muffin pan out of the oven and allow the donut bites to cool down for around 10 minutes before transferring to a wire rack.
- While the donut bites are cooling, make the coating.
- In a bowl, combine the cinnamon and sweetener then mix well.
- In a second bowl, pour the melted butter.
- Dip each of the donut bites into the butter then dredge them in the cinnamon mixture. Make sure to coat each of the donut bites evenly.
- Serve while warm and soft.

7

QUICK KETO LUNCH RECIPES FOR
WHEN YOU'RE ON THE GO

Fig. 10: Lunch, Unsplash, by Bryony Caldwell, 2019,
https://unsplash.com/photos/HQcnr_TgWl/ Copyright 2019 by Bryony
Caldwell/Unsplash.

Following any kind of diet is already a challenge, especially for a diet such as keto. But when you try to encourage your kids to follow the same diet, you need to be more creative in coming up with dishes to keep them happy, healthy, and interested. No matter what time of the day it is or what meal you are serving, going keto doesn't always have to be a struggle. As you have seen, there are different kinds of snacks—both savory and sweet—that you can whip up for your keto kids. But the recipes don't end there.

You can also whip up a number of simple recipes for lunch and dinner to fill your children up and keep them healthy. For this chapter and the next one, we will be going through more complex recipes for heavier meals. The great thing about these recipes is that you can mix and match them according to your meal plans. You can also modify some of these recipes to change the flavors and textures so your kids will keep coming back for more. The more you practice cooking keto meals for yourself, your kids, and the rest of the family, the more you will have the confidence to be more creative with your dishes. So have fun making these yummy recipes with your kids!

KETO BACON AND RANCH PIZZA

Pizza is a favorite among kids and adults alike. As long as you know how to make keto-friendly pizza, you can create different versions to keep your kids and the rest of your family excited. For this recipe, you will be using chicken for the pizza's crust along with a delicious combination of bacon and ranch sauce. It's gluten-free and virtually carb-free. If your kids are craving pizza for lunch, you can make this quick and easy recipe for them... then take a slice for yourself too!

Time: 45 minutes

Serving Size: 1 pizza

Ingredients for the crust:

Fig. 11: Pizza. Pixabay, by Shutterbug75, 2016, https://pixabay.com/photos/american-bacon-barbeque-barbeque-1238698/ Copyright 2016 by Shutterbug75/Pixabay.

- 1 tsp Italian seasoning (keto-friendly)
- ⅓ cup of mozzarella cheese (shredded)
- ⅓ cup of Parmesan cheese (shredded)
- 1 lb ground chicken
- black pepper
- salt

Ingredients for the sauce:

- ⅛ tsp onion powder
- ⅛ tsp salt
- ¼ tsp chives (dried)
- ¼ tsp dill (dried)
- ¼ tsp garlic powder
- ¼ tsp parsley (dried)
- ⅓ cup of avocado mayonnaise
- ⅓ cup of sour cream
- black pepper

Ingredients for the topping:

- 1 cup of mozzarella cheese (shredded, divided into 2)
- 2 medium-sized plum tomatoes (diced)
- 3 slices of bacon (sugar-free, cooked, chopped)

Directions:

- Preheat your oven to 400°F and line a pizza pan with a sheet of parchment paper.
- In a bowl, combine all of the crust ingredients and mix well.
- After combining the crust ingredients, form the mixture into a ball.
- Place the crust ball on the pizza pan, cover it with a sheet of parchment paper, and use a rolling pin to flatten the crust into a big circle.
- After flattening, remove the sheet of parchment paper on top and discard it. If any of the meat mixture gets stuck on the parchment paper, just use a spatula to scrape it off and add it to the crust.
- Place the pizza pan in the oven and bake the crust for about 20 to 25 minutes until the top has browned.

- While baking the crust, add all of the sauce ingredients in a bowl and mix well.
- After baking, take the pizza pan out of the oven, remove the meat crust, flip it over, and remove the sheet of parchment paper.
- Use a spoon to transfer half a cup of the sauce mixture on the crust then spread it to the edges.
- Sprinkle half of the mozzarella cheese over the sauce then top off with tomatoes and bacon.
- Sprinkle the rest of the mozzarella cheese on top.
- Place the pizza back on the pizza pan, return to the oven, and continue baking for about 10 more minutes.
- Take the pizza pan back in the oven and allow the pizza to cool slightly.
- Slice the pizza and serve it while warm with the rest of the ranch sauce.

RAINBOW TACO BOWLS

Have you ever heard about walking tacos? These are easy to eat taco bowls making them perfect for people on-the-go. When you make these walking taco bowls with ingredients of different colors, your kids will surely love eating them. This is another customizable recipe, so you can choose your own ingredients to add to it. Better yet, you can ask your children to help you decide on ingredients by giving them choices of different ingredients with all the colors of the rainbow. Have fun!

Time: 20 minutes

Serving Size: 6 servings

Ingredients:

- 2 tbsp taco seasoning (sugar-free)
- 6 tbsp sour cream
- ⅓ cup of cilantro (fresh, chopped)
- ½ cup of red onion (diced)
- ½ cup of water
- 1 ½ cups of tomato (diced)
- 2 cups of Romaine lettuce (shredded)
- 1 lb ground turkey
- 1 medium-sized avocado (cubed)
- cheese chips (keto-friendly)

Directions:

- In a skillet, add the ground turkey over medium heat and cook for about 10 minutes until brown. Make sure to stir occasionally so you don't burn the turkey.
- Once browned, add the water and taco seasoning then mix until all of the ingredients are well-incorporated. Taste the ground turkey mixture and add more seasoning as needed.
- Bring the mixture to a simmer, turn the heat down to low, and stir-fry the ground turkey mixture for a couple of minutes until the liquid has completely evaporated.
- Break the cheese chips into smaller pieces and place them in a bowl. Place all of the other ingredients in separate bowls.
- Divide the seasoned turkey mixture into small bowls or cups.
- Give each of your kids one bowl or mug with the mixture and allow them to top off their rainbow taco bowls with tomato, red onion, cilantro, lettuce, avocado, cheese chips, and a dollop of sour cream then enjoy while on-the-go!

PIZZA MEATBALLS

These pizza meatballs contain all the good things about pizza in meaty little bites. They're easy to make and they store well too making them perfect for parties, meals, and even for meal preps. Some kids even like to eat these

Fig. 12: Meatballs. Pixabay, by Roundhere44, 2016, https://pixabay.com/photos/meatballs-meat-protein-snack-lunch-4321364/ Copyright 2016 by Roundhere44/Pixabay.

meatballs as a savory snack! You can also pair these pizza meatballs with cauliflower "rice," mashed cauliflower (like mashed potato but you use cauliflower) or even a colorful salad. They're so versatile that you can serve and eat them in different ways!

Time: 35 minutes

Serving Size: 18 to 20 meatballs depending on the size

Ingredients for the meatballs:

- ½ tsp onion powder
- ½ tsp pink salt
- 1 tsp black pepper
- 1 tsp garlic powder
- 1 tbsp oregano
- 3 tbsp almond flour
- 3 tbsp sweet onions (chopped)
- ½ cup of pepperoni slices (chopped)
- 2 lbs ground beef
- 1 large egg
- cooking spray

Ingredients for the sauce:

- ¼ tsp black pepper
- ½ tsp basil (dried)
- ½ tsp garlic powder
- ½ tsp onion powder
- ½ tsp pink salt
- 1 tsp Italian seasoning (keto-friendly)
- 1 tsp oregano (dried)
- 2 tbsp water
- ¾ cup of tomato paste
- 2 cups of tomato sauce

Directions:

- Preheat your oven to 400F and grease a baking sheet with cooking spray.
- In a saucepan, combine all of the sauce ingredients and whisk over medium heat until all of the ingredients are well-incorporated.
- Turn the heat up to high and bring the mixture to a boil. Stir the mixture occasionally while cooking using a wooden spoon.
- Once boiling, turn the heat down to low and allow the sauce to simmer for about 20 minutes.
- Take the saucepan off the heat and set aside while you prepare the meatballs.
- In a separate bowl, combine all of the meatball ingredients and mix everything together until completely combined. If your meatball mixture is too moist, you may add a bit of almond flour.
- Use a spoon to take portions of the meat and shape the portions into balls.
- Place the meatballs in the greased baking sheet leaving an inch of space between them.
- Place the baking sheet in the oven and bake the

meatballs for about 22 to 25 minutes. The baking time depends on the size of your meatballs and the desired doneness.

- Once cooked, take the baking sheet out of the oven and transfer the meatballs to a bowl or serving dish.
- Top the meatballs off with the pizza sauce and serve immediately. You can also serve the meatballs dry with the sauce on the side for dipping.

CHEESY BAKED COD FILLETS

Fish is an essential part of the ketogenic diet as it contains fat (usually healthy fat), protein, and minimal amounts of carbs. When you add cheese to the dish, this makes it more appealing to kids, thus, we have this yummy and healthy recipe. Here, you will be roasting fresh cod fillets with a lovely sauce and savory Parmesan cheese. Then you will have baked fillets that are flaky, tender, cheesy, citrusy, and oh-so-healthy. This dish is low-carb, gluten-free, and it fits right into the ketogenic diet.

Time: 25 minutes

Serving Size: 2 servings

Ingredients for the fish:

- ¼ tsp table salt
- ½ tsp paprika
- 1 tbsp parsley (fresh, chopped)
- ⅓ cup of Parmesan cheese (finely grated)
- 4 cod fillets (fresh, less than 1-inch in thickness)

Ingredients for the sauce:

- 1 tbsp butter (salted)
- 2 tbsp lemon juice (fresh)
- ¼ cup of dry white wine
- 4 cloves of garlic (minced)

Directions:

- Preheat your oven to 400°F and place an oven rack in the middle.
- Use paper towels to pat dry the fresh cod fillets. If you are using frozen cod fillets, make sure to thaw them completely first before patting them dry.
- Season the cod fillets with salt on both sides then set them aside on a plate.
- In an oven-safe pan, add the butter over medium heat. Use a spatula to stir the butter all around for less than a minute until it has melted completely.
- Add the minced garlic to the pan and cook for about 1 to 2 minutes stirring continuously until slightly brown and aromatic.
- Add the lemon juice and white wine to the pan. Stir all of the ingredients together briefly then turn the heat off.
- In a bowl, combine the paprika and Parmesan cheese then mix until well-combined. Set aside.
- Place the seasoned cod fillets in the pan right on top of the sauce.
- Use a spoon to sprinkle the Parmesan cheese mixture over the cod fillets. Make sure that all of the cod fillets are evenly topped with the mixture. Don't worry if any of the Parmesan mixture drops into the sauce as this will just make it taste better.
- Place the pan into the oven and bake the cod fillets for about 15 to 20 minutes until completely cooked

through. You can test the cod fillets by flaking the edge with a fork. If the fillets flake easily, they are already done. If not, continue cooking for about 5 to 10 minutes more.

- Once cooked, take the pan out of the oven and gently transfer the baked cod fillets to plates. Only transfer the cod fillets and leave the sauce in the pan.
- Use a spoon to stir the sauce in the pan so that all the yummy bits are mixed together.
- Drizzle the sauce over each of the cod fillets on the serving plates and serve while hot. Just remind your kids to blow each forkful before eating so they don't burn their mouths.

CRUNCHY CHICKEN TENDERS

Children just love fried chicken and just because they're on keto, this doesn't mean that they cannot have this classic dish. As long as you use keto-friendly ingredients, you can keep serving your kids a wide range of dishes to make them happy without compromising their diet. For this recipe, you have the option to use an air fryer or a frying pan. It all depends on the equipment and appliances that you have in your kitchen. Remember, when it comes to cooking, it's all about creativity and flexibility. The good news is, the more you practice, the easier it becomes for you to make adjustments, modifications, and revisions to recipes as you see fit.

Time: 25 minutes

Serving Size: 8 chicken tenders

Ingredients for the chicken tenders:

- 1 tsp black pepper

- 1 tsp salt
- ¾ cup of almond flour
- 1 ½ cups of pork panko (or any low-carb breading substitute)
- 3 cups of dill pickle juice
- 2 medium-sized eggs (beaten)
- 8 chicken tenders (chicken breast sliced into tenders)
- coconut oil (for frying)

Ingredients for the sauce:

- 1 tsp lemon juice (fresh)
- 2 tsp yellow mustard
- 1 tbsp BBQ sauce (keto-friendly)
- 2 tbsp honey (sugar-free)
- ½ cup of mayonnaise (sugar-free)

Directions:

- In a zip-lock bag, add the pickle juice and chicken tenders then allow them to marinate for a minimum of 1 hour. For best results, marinate the chicken tenders overnight.
- In a bowl, combine the almond flour with salt and pepper then mix well.
- In a second bowl, add the beaten egg.
- In a third bowl, add the pork panko.
- In a sauté pan, add coconut oil over medium heat. Add enough coconut oil to submerge the chicken tenders completely—about 2 inches deep.
- Heat the oil until it reaches a temperature of 350°F. Use a cooking thermometer for this step.
- Once hot enough, start placing the chicken tenders in the oil.

- First, dredge each of the chicken tenders in the almond flour mixture.
- Then dip each of the chicken tenders into the beaten egg making sure that they are all coated evenly.
- Finally, dredge each of the chicken tenders in the pork panko before placing them into the sauté pan.
- Cook each side of the chicken tenders for about 3 minutes until they get a golden brown color. If you plan to cook the chicken tenders in an air fryer, set it to 375°F and cook the chicken tenders for 15 minutes.
- Once cooked, place the chicken tenders on a plate lined with a paper towel to drain any excess oil and cool down slightly.
- While cooling, make the sauce. To do this, combine all of the sauce ingredients in a bowl and mix well.
- Serve the chicken tenders while still warm with the sauce for dipping.

8

DELICIOUS KETO DINNER RECIPES

For a lot of families, dinnertime is when everyone is home and you all have the time to sit together and share a healthy, hearty meal. Therefore, preparing keto-friendly dinner dishes that your kids will also love is the key to encouraging everyone to go keto. If you have already started keto, these recipes will help convince everyone else to follow suit.

Fig. 13: Dinner. Unsplash, by John Fornader, 2019, https://unsplash.com/photos/QlU R-LYK_Wo/ Copyright 2019 by John Fornader/Unsplash.

In this chapter, you will learn how to make some excellent dinner recipes that are completely keto-friendly. Even if you have a picky eater, these tasty recipes will surely appeal to them too. Here's a collection of recipes for you that feature different main ingredients so that you can vary the dishes you serve and keep things interesting for your kids and the rest of the family.

NO NOODLE LASAGNA

Just because your kids are on keto, this doesn't mean that they have to stop eating the classic comfort foods that they love. You can easily make these keto-friendly by changing some ingredients and removing the ones that don't belong to the diet. This is a perfect example of a classic recipe that has been modified to make it keto-friendly. Instead of being a high-carb dish, this no-noodle lasagna will satisfy your kids without making any of you feel guilty about indulging in it.

Time: 50 minutes

Serving Size: 9 servings

Ingredients for the filling:

- 1 tsp garlic powder
- 1 tsp onion powder
- 1 tsp oregano (ground)
- 1 tsp thyme (dried)
- 2 tsp sage (ground)
- ½ cup of Parmesan cheese (grated)
- 2 lbs lean ground beef
- 1 egg (yolk only, beaten)
- black pepper
- salt
- 1 tsp cayenne pepper (optional)

Ingredients for the lasagna:

- ⅛ tsp black pepper
- ¼ tsp garlic powder
- ¼ tsp onion powder
- 1 tbsp olive oil
- ½ cup of Parmesan cheese (grated)
- 1 cup of ricotta cheese
- 1 ¼ cups of spinach
- 2 cups of marinara sauce
- 2 cups of mozzarella cheese (freshly grated)
- 2 eggs (yolks only, beaten)
- parsley (fresh, for garnishing)

Directions:

- Preheat your oven to 450°F.
- In a bowl, combine the garlic powder, onion powder, oregano, thyme, sage, salt, black pepper, and cayenne pepper if desired. Mix well to combine then set aside half a teaspoon for the sauce.
- In a separate bowl, add the ground beef then top off with the seasoning mixture.
- Add the egg yolk and parmesan cheese then mix well until all of the ingredients are well-incorporated.
- Line a baking pan with parchment paper then transfer the ground beef mixture into it. Flatten the mixture using a spatula and make sure that it is evenly spread throughout the baking pan.
- Place the baking pan in the oven and bake the beef mixture for about 7 to 12 minutes.
- Once cooked, take the baking pan out of the oven, drain the excess oil, then slice the cooked beef and set aside.
- Turn down the heat of your oven to 400°F.

- In a bowl, combine the marinara sauce, parmesan cheese, and the reserved seasoning mixture. Mix well then set aside.
- In a separate bowl, beat the eggs then fold the ricotta cheese in. Set aside.
- In a skillet, add the olive oil over medium heat then add the spinach and cook until wilted.
- Season the spinach with garlic powder, black pepper, and onion powder.
- Take the skillet off the heat and start assembling your lasagna.
- Grease a baking pan and add 3 tablespoons of marinara sauce mixture to the bottom. Use a spoon to spread the sauce evenly.
- Top the sauce with the slices of beef then top with more marinara sauce.
- Add the sautéed spinach to the baking pan then top off with the ricotta cheese mixture.
- Sprinkle half of the mozzarella cheese evenly over the top.
- Repeat the last 4 steps using the remaining ingredients making sure that the topmost layer is mozzarella.
- Place the baking pan in the oven and bake the lasagna for about 15 minutes until the top layer has melted and turned slightly golden.
- Once cooked, take the baking pan out of the oven and allow to cool down slightly before slicing and serving.

OVEN-FRIED CRUNCHY FISH

There's nothing more comforting than munching on fried foods for dinner. For this recipe, the fried food is healthy too because you will be using fish and keto-friendly breading. This is a carb-free recipe that

Fig. 14: Fried Fish, Pixabay, by Mogens Petersen, 2017, https://pixabay.com/photos/fish-fish-fillet-breaded-lemon-2302043/ Copyright 2017 by Mogens Petersen/Pixabay.

will surely keep your kids coming back for more. The breading for this recipe can also be used for chicken tenders, pork chops, and other protein sources. This makes the recipe quite versatile–all you have to do is change the protein source to make it a different dish. Then you can serve this with different kinds of keto-friendly dipping sauces for a fun and colorful dining experience.

Time: 45 minutes

Serving Size: 4 servings

Ingredients for the breading:

- ¼ tsp baking powder
- ½ tsp garlic powder
- ½ tsp onion powder
- ½ tsp sea salt
- 1 tsp paprika
- ¼ cup of Parmesan cheese (grated)
- ½ cup of almonds (ground, you can also use almond flour)
- ½ cup of golden flax (ground)
- 2 large eggs

Ingredients for the fish:

- 1 lb white fish fillet (sliced into 8 to 10 pieces)

- ¼ cup of butter (for cooking)

Directions:

- Preheat your oven to 430°F along with a baking sheet. This makes it easier to melt the butter later when you're ready to bake the fish.
- In a bowl, combine all of the breading ingredients except for the eggs then mix until well-incorporated.
- In a second bowl, add the eggs then beat well.
- Dip each of the fish fillet slices into the dry breading mixture making sure to coat them evenly all around.
- Then dip each of the fish fillet slices into the beaten eggs.
- Finally, dip each of the fish fillet slices back into the dry breading mixture. Try to press the fish fillet slices into the breading to coat all sides well. As you finish breading each slice of fish fillet, place them onto a plate.
- Take the preheated baking sheet out of the oven and add half of the butter on it to melt. Spread the butter all over the baking sheet then carefully lay the breaded fish fillet slices on it.
- Place the baking sheet in the oven and bake the breaded fish for about 10 minutes.
- Take the baking sheet out of the oven, flip the breaded fish fillet slices, then drizzle the rest of the butter over them.
- Place the baking sheet back in the oven and continue baking the breaded fish for about 5 to 10 more minutes until completely cooked through and crispy on the outside.
- Take the baking sheet out of the oven and allow the

breaded fish to rest for about 5 minutes before serving.

SAVORY POT ROAST

Pot roasts are an excellent dish for families. They're savory, tender, juicy, and in this case, so easy to make. This keto-friendly recipe only uses 5 ingredients and you can serve it for dinner, for lunch or even as part of your meal prep. If you're having guests over, this savory pot roast is also an excellent dish to serve for a simple yet impressive dish. When making pot roast, aim to choose the best cut of meat so that it will add to the overall taste of the dish. Once you see how easy this dish comes together, it might become one of your go-to recipes for the family.

Time: 1 hour, 50 minutes

Serving Size: 8 servings

Ingredients:

- 2 tbsp beef bouillon
- 2 tbsp ranch seasoning mix (sugar-free, you may use other types of sugar-free seasoning mixes too)
- ½ cup of water
- 3 ½ beef (bottom round roast is best)
- 1 stick of butter (salted)
- 7 Greek pepperoncini peppers

Directions:

- Place the whole roast into an Instant Pot. If you don't own one, a Crock-Pot or a Pressure Cooker works just as well. Just adjust the cooking time as needed.

- Pour the water into a mug and warm it in the microwave for about 1 minute.
- Add the beef bouillon in the warm water and stir until dissolved.
- Sprinkle the ranch seasoning mix all over the roast making sure that the entire surface is seasoned.
- Pour the beef bouillon broth over the roast then top with the peppers and the whole stick of butter.
- Lock the lid of the Instant Pot and make sure to turn the vent on the pot to "seal."
- Select the "Pressure Cooker" setting then cook the roast for 1 ½ hours.
- After the cooking time has passed, allow the Instant Pot to release the pressure normally. This may take around 15 minutes.
- After releasing the pressure, open the lid and carefully transfer the roast to a serving dish.
- Allow the roast to cool down slightly before slicing and serving.

BACON-WRAPPED BAKED PORK CHOPS

Whenever you make these pork chops wrapped in bacon and cook them in the oven, you will always get juicy pork chops each time. Since bacon is high in fat, you won't end up with dry pieces of pork after baking. As long as you follow the instructions of this recipe carefully, you and your kids will enjoy eating it until your plates are empty. If you're a fan of pork chops and you're also a fan of bacon, this will be one of your favorite dishes. It's indulgent, rich, and it fits right into the ketogenic diet.

Time: 50 minutes

Serving Size: 6 servings

Ingredients:

- ¼ tsp onion powder
- ¼ tsp salt
- ½ tsp celery salt
- ½ tsp garlic powder
- 6 pork chops (about 1-inch thick)
- 12 slices of bacon

Directions:

- Line a baking sheet with parchment paper and lay the slices of bacon on it.
- Place the baking sheet in the oven and bake the bacon slices at 425°F for about 10 to 15 minutes. The bacon slices should be cooked but you should still be able to bend them without breaking.
- While the bacon is cooking in the oven, combine the onion powder, salt, celery salt, and garlic powder then mix well.
- Coat the pork chops with the seasoning mixture all over. Make sure that all of the pork chops are lightly and evenly coated with the seasoning mixture. Set aside.
- Take the baking sheet out of the oven and allow the bacon slices to cool down slightly so you can handle them.
- Wrap each of the pork chops with 2 bacon slices each then place them on the baking sheet. Make sure that there are spaces between the pork chops so they don't stick together.
- Place the baking sheet back in the oven and bake the pork chops for about 15 minutes.
- Take the baking sheet out of the oven, turn the pork

chops over, and continue baking for about 10 to 15 minutes more. You can use a meat thermometer to check if the pork chops are done. If the internal temperature of the pork chops is at 145°F, then they are already done.

- Once cooked, take the baking sheet out of the oven and allow the pork chops to cool down slightly before serving.

GRILLED CHICKEN SKEWERS WITH PESTO AVOCADO DIP

This protein-packed dish looks amazing, tastes great, and is really healthy. Just like all the other recipes I have shared with you, it's also really easy to make so you can whip it up for your kids even if you have a busy schedule. You can serve this for dinner or at any other time of the day as it only takes half an hour to cook. The chicken skewers are paired with a creamy dip that's chock-full of healthy fats. This perfect combination makes this dish another star in your arsenal of keto diet recipes.

Time: 30 minutes

Serving Size: 6 servings

Ingredients:

- 2 tbsp lemon juice (freshly squeezed)
- 4 tbsp extra-virgin olive oil
- ¼ cup of pine nuts
- 1 cup of basil leaves (fresh, loosely-packed)
- 1 cup of parsley (fresh, loosely-packed)

Fig. 15: Chicken Skewers. Pixabay, by PH Photos, 2010. https://pixabay.com/photos/shish-kebab-electric-grill-3461/ Copyright 2010 by PD Photos/Pixabay.

- 2 ¼ lbs chicken breasts (boneless, skinless, cut into pieces)
- 1 garlic clove (minced, peeled)
- 1 large avocado (ripe, peeled, cubed)
- zest from 1 lemon
- black pepper
- kosher salt
- olive oil (for grilling)

Directions:

- Preheat your grill pan or outdoor grill for medium heat.
- In a bowl, combine the lemon zest with 1 tablespoon of olive oil and whisk together well.
- Add the pieces of chicken to the mixture then toss until all pieces are evenly coated.
- Season with salt and pepper then continue tossing.
- Thread the chicken pieces onto metal skewers. If you are using bamboo skewers, make sure to soak them in water for 1 hour before starting with the recipe. Set the chicken skewers aside.
- In a skillet, toast the pine nuts over medium heat for about 3 to 4 minutes until they get a light golden color. Toss frequently to avoid burning.
- Once toasted, transfer the pine nuts to a plate to cool.
- In a food processor, combine the toasted pine nuts, parsley, basil, garlic, and a pinch of salt. Process the ingredients until you have a coarse paste.
- Add the lemon juice, avocado, and the rest of the olive oil then continue processing until you get a smooth texture.
- Transfer the dip onto a serving bowl and set aside.
- Brush olive oil onto the preheated grill.

- Place the chicken skewers on the grill for about 5 to 7 minutes until cooked through. Turn the chicken skewers often so they don't burn or stick to the grill.
- Serve the chicken skewers with the pesto avocado dip on the side.

9

KETO DESSERT RECIPES TO SATISFY YOUR CHILDREN'S SWEET TOOTH

Fig. 16: Chocolate. Unsplash, by amirali mirhashemian, 2018, https://unsplash.com/photos/RCVfI8XbYI0/ Copyright 2018 by amirali mirhashemian/Unsplash.

What good is a meal without a sweet treat to end it? For this last chapter of recipes, I will be sharing with you some yummy desserts to make for your kids. As with the lunch and dinner recipes, you can also mix and match these recipes with the sweet snack recipes you have already learned in Chapter 6. To keep your kids interested, you may have to learn how to mix, match, and modify your recipes.

Don't worry, the more you practice cooking, the easier this becomes. Soon, you will become a master chef... at least for your keto kids. With these sweets, your kids don't have to struggle with transitioning from their regular diet to keto. Most kids love sweets so these recipes will surely be the most popular ones for your kids. Enjoy making them!

CHOCO AVOCADO PUDDING

Are you ready for this rich, decadent pudding that's rich in healthy fats and amazing flavors? If you are, then you will surely enjoy making this sweet treat using just a few ingredients and a little bit of time. This dark chocolate dessert will satisfy any sweet tooth and any chocolate craving. It has a perfect texture and an amazing chocolatey taste that your kids might not even believe that it contains healthy avocados!

Time: 5 minutes

Serving Size: 4 servings

Ingredients:

Fig. 17: Pudding. Pixabay, by ElodiV, 2017,
https://pixabay.com/photos/chocolate-mousse-aquafaba-vegan-2695500/ Copyright 2017 by ElodiV/Pixabay.

- 1 tsp stevia drops
- 2 tsp vanilla extract
- ½ cup of almond milk (unsweetened)
- ½ cup of cocoa powder (unsweetened)
- 2 medium-sized avocados (very ripe and soft)
- ½ tsp espresso powder (optional, only add for your servings)

Directions:

- Cut the avocados in half, remove the pits, and use a spoon to scrape out the flesh.
- Place the avocado flesh in a food processor along with the rest of the ingredients. If you want to use espresso powder in your serving of the pudding, mix it in later so your kids don't get the servings with this ingredient.

- Process all of the ingredients together until everything is well-combined and you get a smooth texture without any avocado lumps.
- Transfer the choco avocado pudding into dessert dishes, cover, then place it in the refrigerator to chill before serving.
- Dark cocoa powder works best for this recipe but you can also use normal cocoa powder. For your serving and other adults' servings, you may add espresso powder before chilling to enhance the chocolate taste and make it bolder.
- Serve the chilled pudding after your meal.

COOKIE DOUGH BALLS

Kids love cookie dough and again, just because they're on keto, it doesn't mean they have to stop eating this sweet treat. In fact, while you make this dish with your kids, they might not be able to resist eating the cookie dough right out of the bowl! Just like all the other dishes here, this isn't just for your little ones. The whole family will surely enjoy eating these cookie dough balls right after you make them. Enjoy them as a sweet snack or as a yummy dessert to complete your meals.

Time: 5 minutes

Serving Size: 6 servings

Ingredients:

- ½ tsp vanilla extract
- 2 tbsp keto-friendly sweetener (granulated)
- 5 tbsp butter (softened)
- ½ cup of chocolate chips (sugar-free)
- ¾ cup of cream cheese (softened)

Directions:

- In a bowl with a mixer, combine the butter, cream cheese, vanilla extract, and sweetener.
- Turn the mixer on and mix well until all of the ingredients are well-incorporated.
- Add the chocolate chips and fold them into the mixture using a rubber spatula.
- Use a spoon to take portions of the keto cookie dough then use your hands to form the portions into balls.
- Place the cookie dough balls in an airtight container then place it in the refrigerator to chill it.
- Serve chilled after your meals.

CHOCO COCONUT HAYSTACKS

Here's another chocolatey keto-friendly treat that's so easy to make. This dessert also stores well so you can make a large batch of it and have ready-to-eat desserts for every meal. These choco coconut haystacks fit into the diet because they are completely sugar-free. They are also gluten-free, non-GMO, and even suitable for vegans. The coconut and chocolate are an excellent combination. This dessert is also low-carb as each serving only contains about 2 net carbs. Include this dessert in your meal planning so your kids always have something sweet to look forward to at the end of their meals.

Time: 20 minutes

Serving Size: 14 to 16 haystacks depending on the size

Ingredients:

- 2 tbsp butter

- ½ cup of chocolate chips (sugar-free)
- 1 ½ cups of coconut flakes (unsweetened)

Directions:

- Preheat your oven to 325°F.
- On a cookie sheet, add the coconut flakes and spread them all around in a single layer.
- Place the cookie sheet in the oven and toast the coconut flakes for about 3 minutes.
- Take the cookie sheet out of the oven, stir the coconut flakes around, then place the cookie sheet back in the oven.
- Continue toasting the coconut flakes for about 3 more minutes until they have lightly browned.
- Add water to a double boiler and bring to a boil over medium heat.
- Once boiling, turn the heat down to simmer.
- Add the butter and chocolate chips into the double boiler then stir until all of the chocolate chips have melted completely.
- Add the toasted coconut flakes to the chocolate and fold in using a rubber spatula.
- Line a baking sheet with parchment paper.
- Use a spoon to transfer portions of the choco coconut mixture onto the baking sheet to create your haystacks.
- Place the baking sheet in the refrigerator for about 10 minutes to set before serving.
- Transfer the remaining choco coconut haystacks to an airtight container and store them in the refrigerator to keep them readily available for eating.

STRAWBERRY CHEESECAKE ICE CREAM

Ice cream is the ultimate dessert for the whole family. Once you know how to make ice cream the keto-way, then you can come up with different flavors simply by changing the ingredients. This no-churn ice cream contains healthy and delicious strawberries combined with cream cheese for a luscious and indulgent dessert. In fact, this particular recipe for keto-friendly ice cream is so decadent and rich that you only need to take a few bites to feel fully satisfied. Make a batch of this and see for yourself!

Time: 10 minutes (freezing time not included)

Serving Size: 6 servings

Ingredients:

- ¼ tsp xanthan gum
- 1 tsp vanilla extract
- ½ cup of keto-friendly sweetener (granulated)
- ½ cup of strawberries (frozen or fresh, diced)
- 1 cup of cream cheese
- 1 ½ cups of coconut cream

Fig. 18: Ice Cream. Unsplash, by Ian Dooley, 2017, https://unsplash.com/photos/TLD6i COlybo/ Copyright 2017 by Ian Dooley/Unsplash.

Directions:

- In a bowl with a mixer, combine the cream cheese, and coconut cream.
- Turn the mixer on and mix well until the ingredients are well-incorporated. The chunks of cream cheese should be evenly distributed throughout the mixture.

- Add the xanthan gum, vanilla extract, and sweetener to the mixture then continue mixing until well-combined.
- Add the strawberries to the mixture and fold in using a spatula.
- Transfer the mixture into a loaf pan or any other ice cream container and place it in the freezer.
- Freeze the strawberry cheesecake ice cream for at least 2 hours before serving. The longer you freeze it, the firmer the ice cream becomes.
- You can follow the same steps for making different cheesecake ice cream flavors. Just replace the strawberry with other ingredients and you're good to go!

JELLY ROLL-UPS

Jello is fun, colorful, and you can use it to make this unique and special treat. This is a fun dessert for your kids to eat and it's really fun to make too. Whip this up for your kids and you can even make larger batches for parties and other celebrations. If you need a fun type of food to serve, this is one of the best options. You can even use different flavors of Jello to create jelly roll-ups of different colors. Let your children pick the color so they will feel more excited to help you make this easy dessert.

Time: 20 minutes

Serving Size: 1 jelly roll log

Ingredients:

- 2 tbsp water
- ⅓ cup of heavy cream

- 1 pack of Jello (sugar-free, any flavor)
- cooking spray

Directions:

- Set aside ⅕ teaspoon of the Jello powder.
- Grease a baking pan with cooking spray. The oil you use shouldn't have any flavors (like coconut or avocado for example) and make sure that the whole inside of the baking pan is lightly coated.
- In a microwave-safe bowl, add the heavy cream and heat for about 20 to 30 seconds until hot.
- Add the rest of the Jello powder to the hot cream then mix well until all the powder has dissolved completely.
- Pour the cream and Jello mixture into the greased pan making sure that it covers the whole bottom. Swirl the liquid around a bit to make an even layer.
- Place the pan in the refrigerator for about 10 minutes until the Jello sets.
- In a microwave-safe bowl, heat the water for a few seconds until hot.
- Add the remaining Jello powder then mix well until it's completely dissolved.
- Take the pan out of the refrigerator then pour the water and Jello mixture over the Jello and cream later.
- Swirl the pan around to ensure that the top layer covers the whole surface of the bottom layer evenly.
- Place the pan back in the refrigerator and allow both Jello layers to set completely for at least 15 minutes.
- Once set, take the pan out of the refrigerator.
- Use a scraper to lift one side of the Jello layers then

start rolling it gently into a log. Do this while it's still in the pan so the Jello layers don't break apart.

- Once you have rolled an entire log, gently place the Jello log on a sheet of food-grade plastic wrap then wrap the log tightly.
- Place the Jello log back in the refrigerator to set and chill.
- When you're ready to serve, use a knife to cut the log up into Jelly roll-up slices that are about half-an-inch thick. Enjoy!

10

LET YOUR CHILD HELP YOU COOK!

Fig. 19: Kids Cooking. Pixabay, by Andrzej Rembowski, 2019, https://pixabay.com/photos/cooking-lesson-workshops-children-4283413/ Copyright 2019 by Andrzej Rembowski/Pixabay.

Cooking is a basic life skill and if you can teach this to your child early on, they may develop a love for it. Even children as young as 3 years old can learn how to cook or at least help you out with simple tasks while you cook for them. One of the most effective ways to encourage your child to follow the ketogenic diet is to involve them in the cooking process. So if you want your child to succeed on keto, get them involved!

It might seem intimidating at first, especially when you think about all the dangerous things that can be found in your kitchen. But as long as you teach your child how to handle kitchen utensils and appliances properly, you can help your child protect themselves from these potential dangers. If you're wondering why you should allow your child to help you out in the kitchen, here are some important reasons for you to consider:

1. Cooking allows you to talk to your child about health

When you cook your meals at home, you can ensure that everything you eat is healthy. In the same way, when you cook your child's meals at home and involve them in the process, you can make sure that everything your child eats is healthy and keto-friendly. While you cook with your child, this would be the perfect time to start talking about health. Start by telling your child what you will be cooking. Then introduce different ingredients to your child as you prepare the meal.

For each cooking session, you can teach one skill to your child. For instance, you can start with washing vegetables. This is a very easy task that even a young child can do. Then you can describe what you are doing at each step while your child watches you with the more difficult tasks. Think of it as having your own cooking show with your child as your audience. Throughout the process, talk about what it means to be healthy, why you have chosen certain ingredients for the meal you're preparing, and why your child should prioritize their health too.

2. Your child learns how to use their senses

Aside from having fun, children also learn more effectively when they can use all of their senses—and there is no other activity that engages all of the senses completely like cooking. Your child can see, touch, and smell the ingredients while preparing them. Then as you are cooking the dish, you can let your child continue using these senses along with their taste and hearing. They can listen to the sounds you make while cooking and you can let them taste the dish at every step. From start to finish, cooking is an immersive experience that involves all the senses which is why it's an excellent activity for your child to learn.

3. Cooking enhances your child's language development

As you talk about health, healthy ingredients, and the different steps of the cooking process, you are also building your child's vocabulary. Through these explanations and conversations, you are honing your child's language skills by teaching them new words, sequencing, and even new concepts. Simple as this activity might seem, it can also teach your child comprehension as you converse while you cook together.

4. Cooking can help your child understand math concepts

When you follow recipes, you will always use measurements to make the dishes correctly. Teach these measurements to your child and you will also be reinforcing their math skills. Cooking involves rote counting, number recognition, and different types of mathematical language as you measure the ingredients to use for your dishes. You can even introduce the concept of time since a lot of recipes require specific cooking times to complete the dishes.

5. Cooking can help your child become interested in science and creativity

Your kitchen is like a Science Lab where you can perform experiments with your child through cooking. Show your child how ingredients change in color, texture, and form as you cook them. You can even ask your child to make observations and predictions, especially when you are cooking new dishes. After your child has tried cooking for some time, then you can ask them to think of their own recipes. This allows them to unleash their creativity while having fun creating dishes that they will also be eating.

THE BENEFITS OF TEACHING CHILDREN HOW TO COOK THEIR OWN MEALS

Whether you love cooking or this is your first time to really learn how to cook, involving your child in the process can be beneficial to them in different ways. Your main goal for involving your child in the cooking process is to encourage them to accept the ketogenic diet more openly and encourage them to follow it happily. Children love it when their parents allow them to do "grown-up things," especially while they are young. As they watch you cook in the kitchen, they feel the urge to do the same things as you're doing and if you invite them to help, this will surely make your child excited.

Most adults who don't know how to cook or who don't have any interest in it weren't exposed to this skill while they were still young. Children can learn basic kitchen skills and the earlier you teach them, the more they will learn as they grow up. In fact, when you expose your child to cooking early on, they will also learn how to keep themselves safe while in the kitchen. Here are the other benefits to look forward to when you involve your child in the cooking process:

1. It encourages your child to try new things

When you involve your child in cooking, you are also exposing them to different types of food. This is an amazing learning experience for children as you can teach them all about fresh fruits, vegetables, meat, poultry, and other ingredients that you will use for your dishes. When your child is exposed to these ingredients and you also allow them to use their senses to explore those ingredients, then they will be more willing to try new things when you offer them. This exploration works in two ways as it also cultivates in your child an open-minded and welcoming approach to food. This, in turn, may encourage your child to become more adventurous in terms of trying out new dishes. When this happens, the new diet you are trying to get your child to follow becomes much easier.

2. It helps develop their fine motor skills

Cooking involves a lot of skills like rolling, measuring, spreading, squeezing, slicing, and more. These skills help develop your child's hand-eye and fine-motor skills. These are very important skills children have to learn to help them excel in school. Try to match the skills to the age of your child. Don't assign a skill that is too easy or too difficult for your child. If the task is too easy, your child might think that you don't trust them to do more challenging things. If the task is too difficult, your child might get frustrated and this might affect their self-esteem. Start with simple tasks and when you think your child is ready, give them more challenging tasks to master. Soon, they might start asking you to try out different things. As long as you're there to guide them, allow your child to try these things so their interest in cooking will keep growing.

3. It improves their attention and focus

While you and your child are cooking, you need to pay attention to each task as you work through it. Emphasize the importance of focusing on these tasks so that your child will learn to do the same thing. This is especially important if you start assigning your child with tasks that come with an element of danger like slicing, adding ingredients to a pot or even handling hot things like freshly-baked cookies. Although you won't be teaching such tasks to young children, honing their attention and focus through simpler tasks prepares them to handle more complex things as they grow older.

4. It gives you a chance to strengthen your relationship

Each time you cook a new dish with your child, this gives you a chance to spend quality time together. As you explain things to your child, you are conversing with them while imparting valuable knowledge. Cooking together can help strengthen your relationship, especially if you keep things positive and you don't scold your child when they aren't picking up a skill as fast as you want them too. When you cook with your child, prepare to spend more time on the process. You have to be more aware and more patient so that your child learns from the process instead of getting traumatized by it.

5. It helps your children become more confident

As you give your child responsibilities, this will make them more confident in their abilities. In the beginning, your child might feel fearful, especially when you give them complex tasks. But when you encourage them and guide them through it, they will discover that they can complete those complex tasks. This discovery comes with a heightened sense of confidence that they can apply to the different aspects of their life too.

6. It's fun!

Finally, cooking is a lot of fun! Everything is colorful, exciting, and new. When you welcome your child to help you cook, they will already feel happy and excited. When you make the process positive for your child, it will surely become fun for them. Once your dishes are done, your child will also feel excited to eat what you have cooked together, no matter how unfamiliar it is! Again, this will make it easier for you to encourage your child to continue following the ketogenic diet.

TIPS FOR LETTING YOUR CHILDREN COOK WITH YOU

By now, you already know why you should involve your child in cooking and how this activity can benefit them. With all of this information in mind, it's time to start involving your child in the task. Just as you would introduce the ketogenic to your child, introduce cooking in a positive way. Don't treat this like a chore or something that you HAVE to do to make your child happy. Instead, think of it as a learning experience for both of you. As you teach your child essential skills and encourage them to follow the keto diet, you are also learning new things about your child. Cooking with kids is an enriching activity that will make you happier, healthier, and closer to each other.

Before you start involving your child in cooking, give them time to observe you first. Allowing your child to watch you cook will increase their interest in the task. When your child has any questions for you, answer them happily. Then the clincher would be when you announce to your child that you will start allowing them to help you cook meals! Here are some pointers for you to start with as you involve your child in this essential task:

1. Be patient with your child

When you involve your child in the process of cooking, accept that the process will take more time. You will have to teach your child a new skill then wait for them to accomplish the task that involves the skill. Then you would also have to take the time to explain things to your child and answer all of their questions. All of these things will add up to the time it takes for you to cook. Try not to rush your child through the process. Instead, start to cook earlier so you can still eat your meals at the scheduled time.

2. Prepare your kitchen when it's time to involve your child

During the planning stage of your meal prep, include simple recipes where you can involve your child in the cooking process. Make a mark on your plan to indicate that this is the recipe that you will ask your child to help you cook. When it's time for you to cook with your child, make sure to prepare your kitchen first. Layout all of the ingredients, all of the tools you need, and study the recipe beforehand. That way, you can guide your child throughout the cooking process without having to keep referring to your recipe as this might cause more delay.

When cooking with your child, it's best to use regular kitchen utensils. This is the best way to teach your child how to use these utensils correctly and safely. Also, you can teach your child the names of these different utensils to get them familiar. When you want to teach your child how to slice fruits and veggies, you can allow them to use a real knife. For the first few times, you can hold their hands to show them how to hold the knife and how to slice properly. For tasks like these, focus all of your attention on your child. Don't do anything else while they accomplish the task. Do this to help reduce the risk of your child getting injured.

3. Consider your child's age and abilities

When teaching your child to cook and help out in the kitchen, you should always consider their age and abilities. For instance, you should never introduce slicing when your child is only 3 years old and it's their first time to help out. Or if you have an older child, you shouldn't just give them the task of washing vegetables over and over again as they will probably get bored. While it's best to start with simple tasks, you should move on to more complex tasks over time to keep things interesting. To give you an idea of the common skills that you can assign to your child depending on their age, here are some standard guidelines:

For children 2 to 5 years old

- Rinsing vegetables and fruits.
- Stirring ingredients in a bowl.
- Measuring liquid and solid ingredients.
- Mashing soft ingredients.
- Snapping beans in half.
- Cutting soft ingredients using a blunt knife.
- Helping you get ingredients.
- Pouring liquids from one container to another.
- Using a cookie cutter to cut shapes out.

For children 6 to 8 years old

All of the cooking skills above plus:

- Measuring ingredients.
- Kneading dough.
- Using their hands to form patties and cookies.
- Peeling garlic and onions.
- Peeling other types of vegetables.
- Grating cheese.
- Spreading peanut butter, frosting, butter or soft cheese with a butter knife.
- Chopping semi-soft ingredients using a steak knife with a rounded end.

- Setting the table.

For children 9 to 12 years old

All of the cooking skills above plus:

- Planning meals for the week.
- Going through recipes and following the instructions.
- Slicing ingredients with a chef's knife.
- Using a garlic press to squeeze garlic.
- Grating harder ingredients like vegetables.
- Opening cans.
- Cooking soup.
- Placing food in the oven and taking them out while wearing oven mitts.
- Baking simple pastries.
- Using a food processor.
- Using other simple kitchen appliances like the microwave, blender, and electric mixer.
- Powering on the stove element and setting the temperature of the oven (under your supervision).

For teenagers 14 to 16 years old

All of the cooking skills above plus:

- Buying the ingredients you need for the recipes using a shopping list as a reference.
- Marinating meat, poultry, and fish.
- Using all of the other appliances in your kitchen under your supervision.
- Using the stovetop on their own.
- Heating food in the microwave on their own.

- Taking baking sheets and baking trays out of the oven while wearing oven mitts.
- Learning how to dice, mince, and chop using different types of knives.
- Using a colander to drain cooked pasta.
- Pan-frying and sautéing ingredients.

4. Orient your child before you start

After preparing everything you need for your cooking session, it would be very helpful for you to explain the whole process of cooking from start to finish. Start by identifying the ingredients or asking your child to identify them for you. Then identify the tools you will use one by one. The next thing to explain are the safety rules when cooking (we will discuss these in the next section). After that, you can start explaining each of the steps as you do them. Going through all of these steps is important as it makes things clearer for your child. However, these steps do take time which is why it's better for you to start cooking early so your mealtimes don't get delayed.

5. Give your child important tasks

When you have a planned cooking session with your child, make sure to involve them in it completely. Don't just give them an easy task then do everything else yourself. Children know when you're brushing them off and they also know when you're genuinely including them. If you want your child to gain confidence, be more enthusiastic, and feel more excited about their diet, give them important tasks to do. This sense of responsibility will make your child feel happier and more proud after they've accomplished the task you assigned to them.

6. Don't stress when your child makes a mess

Cooking with children won't be as neat and tidy as cooking on your own. Expect your cooking session to be messy, especially during the first few tries. As long as your child isn't purposely making a mess, just allow things to unfold. Then when you're done with the dish, you can tidy up the kitchen together.

7. Allow your child to choose what recipes to cook

When you feel like your child has already gotten the hang of cooking and they're enjoying it, you can take things further by allowing them to choose which recipe to cook together. Do this while you are meal planning. Allow your child to go through your recipe book and let them choose which recipe to cook. Just make sure to schedule this recipe when you have a lot of time to make it together.

8. Make it an enjoyable learning experience

As you apply all of these tips and the things you learn along the way, always try to make each cooking experience an enjoyable learning experience. That way, your child will always want to cook with you even though this only happens a few times a week. The more enjoyable your cooking sessions are, the more your child will love spending this special time with you.

ALWAYS PUT SAFETY FIRST

To ensure that your child will succeed on the ketogenic diet, try to encourage them to become a more adventurous eater. This diet isn't just about convincing your child to eat their greens. Since it's quite restrictive, there are several things you would have to do to transition your child from their current diet to keto. One of the most effective ways to do this is by involving your child in the cooking process. Now that you have enough tips and strategies to get your child to help you in the kitchen, it's time to go through the most important part of the process—safety.

For you and your child to enjoy your cooking sessions, you must make sure that you both put safety first. This is very important as you don't want your child to end up getting hurt or injured while cooking. If this happens, it might sour your child to the whole experience. Aside from supervising your child, you should also teach them how to work in the kitchen safely. From the simplest tasks to the most complex ones, safety should always be your priority. When your child learns how to prioritize safety, you won't have to worry about them even when you leave them to accomplish tasks on their own. Teaching your child safety also makes them feel more confident as they see that you allow them to handle things on their own. Here are the basic safety tips to teach your children when cooking in the kitchen:

Wash your hands first

Before you start preparing ingredients or cooking dishes, you must wash your hands first. Emphasize the importance of washing your hands first as it ensures food safety. Talk about how we all tend to touch different things that often have germs on them. Then ask your child if they want those germs to get into their food. Of course, your child will probably tell you that they don't want any germs to get into the food that you will cook together.

After explaining the importance of hand-washing, show your child how to wash your hands properly then guide them as they wash their own hands. You may have to do this a couple of times before your child learns the proper way of washing their hands. Then make this the first step of each of your cooking sessions as part of your safety measures.

Clean up as you work

While you and your child are cooking, teach them how to clean up messes and spills to avoid slips or falls. Think about it: if some kind of liquid spills on the floor and your child steps on it, they might slip and get hurt. Again, explain the reason for cleaning up messes and spills so your child understands why you're taking these extra steps while cooking. Also, cleaning up as you work makes it easier for you to clean up the whole kitchen after your cooking session.

When holding hot items, use protective gear

Explain to your child why they should never touch hot items as they will get burned if they do. Potholders and oven mitts are the best things to use when handling hot pans, pots or even appliances. Show your child how to don these protective items to prevent burns and other injuries.

Teach your child how to use knives properly

One of the most dangerous things in the kitchen is a knife and the sharper a knife is, the more dangerous it can be. Knife skills are very important when cooking, therefore, you would have to teach these skills to your child sooner or later. It's okay for your child to learn how to use knives properly. The key here is to show them how to use knives properly and guide them as they practice. Also, while your child practices their knife skills, you should always be there to supervise. Only when your child is old enough and has gained proficiency in using knives should you allow them to handle this kitchen item on their own.

Tell your child to always ask permission first before they do any cooking

As you involve your child in the process of cooking, they

might feel very excited to keep practicing their cooking skills. If you see this enthusiasm in your child, that's okay. Just tell your child that they should always ask permission from you first before trying to prepare or cook anything in the kitchen. If they want to make simple snacks on their own, allow them to do this under your supervision. That way, you can always remind them of the basic safety tips while they try to whip up simple dishes on their own.

When it comes to cooking, safety is key. As long as you can teach these basic safety tips to your child along with any other safety tips you can think of, you can keep cooking with your child which, in turn, makes them more excited to follow their new ketogenic diet.

CONCLUSION

MAKING THE KETOGENIC DIET FUN
AND EASY FOR YOUR CHILDREN

Fig. 20: Cheers to Keto. Unsplash, by Pablo Merchán Montes, 2018,
https://unsplash.com/photos/wYOPqmtDDow/ Copyright 2018 by
Pablo Merchán Montes/Unsplash.

There you have it! Everything you need to know to start your child on keto.

As you can see, the ketogenic diet isn't as simple as it may seem, especially when you plan to encourage your child to follow it. If you aren't following the ketogenic diet yet, then you may want to consider following it first for a few months so that you can experience it for yourself and share your experiences with your child when you start them on the diet too. If you're already on keto and you want your child to follow the same diet so they can experience the benefits too, then you may start right away! After all, you already learned a wealth of information about how you can help your child begin their own keto journey.

From the start of this eBook, I have shared with you some important facts and tips about keto for kids. In the first chapter, we started off by defining the keto diet and discovering why there is so much hype surrounding it right now. Then we focused on whether this diet is suitable or even safe for children. As we have previously established, the keto diet is safe as long as you make sure that your child follows it correctly. Then we moved on to some practical and effective tips to start your child on keto and how you can help them stick with the diet by keeping them inspired and motivated.

In the next chapter, we focused on the good and bad sides of keto. I wanted to include this information so that you can see both sides of the coin. Only learning about the benefits and advantages of the ketogenic diet might cause you a lot of problems because you wouldn't know if your child is already experiencing the side effects or risks of this diet. It's important to know the good and the bad so that you know exactly what to expect and what you need to do when you start seeing the side effects in your child. As I have been emphasizing throughout this eBook, your child's safety should always be your priority.

Then I shared with you several tips, tricks, and strategies for meal preps. As per experience, I believe that meal preps can help make your child transition into the keto diet easier. Through meal preps, you can make sure that your child is always eating keto-friendly food no matter what time of the day it is, whether they are at home or in school. Of course, this chapter wouldn't make much sense unless you have recipes to include in your meal prep, right?

This is why the next 5 chapters are where I shared with you some of the tastiest, easiest, and healthiest recipes to start your child on keto. As you may have noticed, these recipes are so simple that you can follow them even if this is your first time cooking on keto. These recipes are some of my daughter's favorites and I hope your child will love them too.

Finally, the last chapter of this book focused on how you can involve your child in cooking their keto meals. Involving them in this process makes them more willing to try new foods and it also keeps them motivated to follow the diet long-term.

As promised, I have shared with you the fundamentals of the keto diet for kids plus a number of scrumptious recipes for you to try out. Guiding your child through a new diet might not be the easiest thing to do but I am sure that you can do it with everything you have learned here. Thank you very much for downloading and reading my eBook and I hope you enjoyed reading it as much as I enjoyed writing it. If you want other parents to learn the same things you did, then please leave a favorable review. That way, you would have played a role in helping other parents who want to help their own children start the ketogenic diet too. Good luck with your new endeavor and don't forget to have fun with it!

REFERENCES

6-Ingredient Veggie Egg Cups Tutorial {Gluten-Free, Keto, Low Carb}. (2019). Retrieved from https://recipesfroma-pantry.com/egg-cups/

Abesamis, A. (2019). Why You Should Never, Ever Put Your Kid On The Keto Diet. Retrieved from https://www.huff-post.com/entry/kids-keto-safe_l_5d5ae55de4b036065b6a9aea

AboutKidsHealth. (n.d.). Retrieved from https://www.aboutkidshealth.ca/article?contentid=2099&language=english

AMAZING DELICIOUS Keto Pull Apart Pizza Bread Recipe! (2019). Retrieved from https://www.isavea2z.-com/keto-pull-apart-pizza-bread-recipe/

Baked Cod (Low Carb, Keto). (2018). Retrieved from https://www.savorytooth.com/baked-cod/

Ball, R. (2019). Creamy Keto OREO Cookies and Cream Fat Bombs. Retrieved from https://www.forkly.-

com/recipes/creamy-keto-oreo-cookies-and-cream-fat-bombs/

Banz, J. (2019). Edible Keto Cookie Dough. Retrieved from https://jenniferbanz.com/edible-cookie-dough

Banz, J. (2017). Low Carb Ice Cream - Strawberry Cheesecake. Retrieved from https://jenniferbanz.com/low-carb-no-churn-ice-cream

Barot, M. (2017). Keto Pigs In A Blanket: Make Snack Time Fun Again! Retrieved from https://www.ketoconnect.net/keto-pigs-in-a-blanket/

Billis, S. (2018). The 6 Best Meal-Planning Tips for Busy Moms Who Aren't Meal Planners. Retrieved from https://www.workingmother.com/6-best-meal-planning-tips-for-busy-moms-who-arent-meal-planners

Blades, N. (2019). Some Parents Are Putting Their Kids On Keto Diets. Retrieved from https://www.womenshealthmag.com/weight-loss/a28651268/keto-for-kids/

Bragg, M. C. (2019). Keto for Kids! Retrieved from https://www.guitarpedalsonline.com/2019/07/25/keto-for-kids/

Brekken, C. A. (n.d.). About the Keto Diet. Retrieved from http://blogs.oregonstate.edu/oregonketokids/aboutketodiet/

Broccoli Cheese Nuggets - Low Carb, Grain Gluten Free, THM S. (2019). Retrieved from https://joyfilledeats.com/broccoli-cheese-nuggets/

Can my kids do keto too? (n.d.). Retrieved from https://www.ruled.me/faq/can-my-kids-do-keto-too/

Cooking safety rules for kids. (n.d.). Retrieved from

https://www.childrens.com/health-wellness/cooking-safety-rules

Dell'antonia, K., & Laskey, M. (2015). Cooking With Kids: 5 Reasons You Should Be Doing It. Retrieved from https://www.nytimes.com/2015/09/03/dining/cooking-with-kids-5-reasons-you-should-be-doing-it.html

Dionne, S. (2016). 10 tips to cook with your kids and have fun! Retrieved from https://www.arcticgardens.ca/blog/tips-cooking-with-kids/

Fernando, N. (n.d.). 5 Great Reasons to Cook with Your Kids. Retrieved from https://www.healthychildren.org/English/healthy-living/nutrition/Pages/Cooking-With-Your-Children.aspx

Godinez, B. (2018). Ketosis for Children: Pros & Cons. Retrieved from https://perfectketo.com/ketosis-for-children/

Goodwin, M. (2018). 7 Tips for Teaching Children to Cook. Retrieved from https://www.frugalandthriving.com.au/teach-children-to-cook/

Grilled Chicken with Avocado Pesto. (2017). Retrieved from https://www.foodnetwork.com/recipes/food-network-kitchen/grilled-chicken-with-avocado-pesto-3796532

Hire , C. (n.d.). Top 10 tips for cooking with kids. Retrieved from https://www.bbcgoodfood.com/howto/guide/top-10-tips-cooking-kids

Is keto safe for kids? (n.d.). Retrieved from https://www.childrens.com/health-wellness/is-keto-safe-for-kids

Is Keto Safe for Kids? Here's What You Need to Know.

(2018). Retrieved from https://hip2keto.com/tips/keto-safe-kids/

Jello Roll Ups. (2019). Retrieved from https://ketocook.com/2012/09/17/jello-roll-ups/

Kapsalis, A. (2019). Keto for children - Everything you need to know. Retrieved from https://www.greekgoesketo.com/keto-for-children-everything-you-need-to-know/

Keto for Kids. (n.d.). Retrieved from https://highfatchan.com/keto-for-kids/

Keto for Kids - Practical Tips & Advice from Busy Mums. (2019, August 19). Retrieved from https://havebutterwilltravel.com/keto-for-kids/

Keto For Kids: Is It Safe For Kids To Be Low Carb Too? (2019). Retrieved from https://imsimplyadad.com/keto-for-kids/

Keto for Kids: Is Keto Safe for Children?: Ketoned Bodies Keto for Kids: Is Keto Safe for Children? (2019). Retrieved from https://ketonedbodies.com/keto-for-kids/

Keto Recipes for Kids - Keen for Keto - Kid Friendly Keto Meals! (2020). Retrieved from https://keenforketo.com/keto-recipes-for-kids-2/

Ketogenic Diet for Kids. (2014). Retrieved from https://www.chop.edu/treatments/ketogenic-diet

Ketogenic Diet: Is It Really Worth the Hype? (n.d.). Retrieved from https://8fit.com/nutrition/ketogenic-diet-is-it-really-worth-the-hype/

Ketogenic Diet: Treating Children's Seizures with Food. (2020). Retrieved from https://www.healthychildren.org/English/health-issues/conditions/seizures/Pages/Ketogenic-Diet.aspx

Kids and Food: 10 Tips for Parents (for Parents) - Nemours KidsHealth. (2015). Retrieved from https://kidshealth.org/en/parents/eating-tips.html

Kids and Keto. (2018). Retrieved from https://intermoun-tainhealthcare.org/blogs/topics/pediatrics/2018/04/kids-and-keto/

Kitchen Safety Tips for Kids. (n.d.). Retrieved from https://www.childrenscolorado.org/conditions-and-advice/parenting/parenting-articles/kitchen-safety-tips/

Krampf, M. (2017). Keto Low Carb Peanut Butter Protein Balls Recipe - 4 Ingredients. Retrieved from https://www.wholesomeyum.com/recipes/keto-low-carb-peanut-butter-protein-balls-recipe/

Krampf, M. (2020). How To Make a Walking Taco Bowl - Recipe for a Crowd or Weeknight. Retrieved from https://www.wholesomeyum.com/walking-taco-bowl-recipe/

Lopa, J. (2015). Jessica Lopa. Retrieved from https://mommyuniversitynj.com/2015/03/16/10-benefits-of-cooking-with-kids/

Low Carb Donut Bites with Apple and Cinnamon. (2020). Retrieved from https://stepawayfromthecarbs.com/low-carb-donut-bites/

Low-Carb Kids - how to start and is it healthy? What to eat? (2019). Retrieved from https://www.ditchthecarbs.com/kids/

MarcAurele, L. (2019). Bacon Wrapped Pork Chops Recipe.

Retrieved from https://lowcarbyum.com/bacon-wrapped-pork-chops-recipe/

MarcAurele, L. (2019). Keto Chocolate Avocado Pudding (Paleo). Retrieved from https://lowcarbyum.com/dark-chocolate-avocado-pudding/

MarcAurele, L. (2020). Stevia Keto Meringue Cookies Recipe. Retrieved from https://lowcarbyum.com/egg-fast-sugar-free-meringue-cookies/

MarcAurele, L. (2020). Keto Lasagna with Spinach and Meat. Retrieved from https://lowcarbyum.com/keto-lasagna-meatza-layers/

MarcAurele , L. (2020). Bacon Ranch Keto Chicken Crust Pizza. Retrieved from https://lowcarbyum.com/bacon-ranch-chicken-crust-pizza/

Martin, A. (2017). The Busy Mom's Guide to Meal Planning. Retrieved from https://www.thesimpledollar.com/save-money/busy-moms-guide-to-meal-planning/

McCrary, A. (2018). The Best Whole30 Pizza Meatballs. Retrieved from https://healthylittlepeach.-com/2018/11/02/pizza-meatballs/

McNelis, K. (2012). 5 meal planning tips for busy moms. Retrieved from https://thefamilyfreezer.-com/2012/09/20/5-meal-planning-tips-for-busy-moms/

Mullens, A. (2020). Can a low-carb diet help with ADHD? Retrieved from https://www.dietdoctor.com/low-carb/adhd-autism

Preiato, D. (2019). Keto for Kids: Appropriate Uses, Adverse Effects, and Safety. Retrieved from https://www.healthline.-com/nutrition/keto-for-kids

Rizzo, N. (n.d.). The Keto Meal Plan for Moms. Retrieved from https://www.parents.com/recipes/healthyeating/moms/the-keto-meal-plan-for-moms/

Sadler, A. (2019). The Fuel-Good, Keto-Happy Shopping List for Beginners. Retrieved from https://www.healthline.com/health/food-nutrition/keto-shopping-list

Scott-Dixon, K., & Kollias, H. (2019). The Ketogenic Diet: Does it live up to the hype? The pros, the cons, and the facts about this not-so-new diet craze. Retrieved from https://www.precisionnutrition.com/ketogenic-diet

Seelinger, M. (2018). Keto Fried Chicken Tenders Chick-Fil-A Copycat Recipe. Retrieved from https://www.meganseelinger.com/blog/ketofriedchicken-tenders

Slyter, K. (2019). 8 Proven Tips on How to Get Kids to Eat Healthy. Retrieved from https://www.rasmussen.edu/degrees/education/blog/how-to-get-kids-to-eat-healthy/

Smith, D. S. (2019). Ninja Foodi Pressure Cooker Pot Roast Recipe. Retrieved from https://drdavinahseats.com/recipes/keto-recipes/ninja-foodi-pressure-cooker-pot-roast

Start Here. (2019). Retrieved from https://www.fourscore-living.com/low-carb-chocolate-chip-muffins/

The Benefits of Cooking with Kids. (2019). Retrieved from https://www.healthylittlefoodies.com/the-benefits-of-cooking-with-kids/

The Best Low Carb Oven Fried Fish: THM S. (2018). Retrieved from https://www.wholesomerecipebox.com/low-carb-oven-fried-fish/

Top 10 Keto Ingredients: High Fat Low Carbohydrate Ingredients. (2020). Retrieved from https://www.culinarynutrition.com/top-10-keto-ingredients/

Top 7 Kitchen Safety Tips To Teach Your Kids. (2019). Retrieved from https://www.superhealthykids.com/parenting/kitchen-safety-rules-kids/

Trenum, K. (2019). Coconut Haystack Recipe (Keto /Low Carb). Retrieved from https://kaseytrenum.com/coconut-haystacks-keto-low-carb/

Weaver, R. (2019). Keto for Kids: 4 Reasons Why Your Children Might Need It. Retrieved from https://www.ketogenic-supplementreviews.com/blog/keto-for-kids/

Wulfers, K. (n.d.). Your Kids Are Going to Eat These Cheddar Cauli-Tots Like You Can't Imagine. Retrieved from https://www.yummymummyclub.ca/blogs/katja-wulfers-around-the-table/20150309/cauliflower-cheese-recipes